POETRY NOW

SECOND TIME SINGLE

1993

Edited by Veronica Hannon

First published in Great Britain in 1993 by
POETRY NOW
1-2 Wainman Road, Woodston,
Peterborough, PE2 7BU

All Rights Reserved

Copyright Contributors 1993

FOREWORD

One of the most difficult things about writing a foreword for this book was the fact that this subject is known to all of us. Sometime during our lives or perhaps frequently, we have all known or initiated the trauma of rejection. How many times have we all sat there debating whether to ring, write a letter or bravely tackle the subject face to face?

Some of us manage to be tactful, sometimes it takes scathing wit to penetrate the barriers that we all erect to counteract rejection. Either way the dreaded words of 'I've found someone else' or 'Lets just be friends' are constantly in our minds when we set out on the perilous road of relationships.

All the writers in this anthology tell their own tales, either from being on the receiving end or the bliss of having found freedom. There were many times whilst selecting the poems for this collection that I have found myself laughing or moaning in recognition.

Whether the saga is that the Gold Blend adverts or those of one night stands there is always a hint of humour or a telling insight which makes this book a compulsive read.

The poets in this anthology come from all over the country and from all walks of life. What unites them is that they have all suffered the hardships of breaking up and survived to tell the tale and they tell it well. Whether writing in blank verse or carefully constructed rhyme, with sparkling wit or with cruel perception the poems between these covers will strike a telling chord with everyone.

Contents

The Row	Heather SMith	1
Jumped Upon	Maureen Weldon	2
Window Gazing	Rosalyn Carr	3
After the Masked Ball the Dirty Dancing	Geoff Stevens	4
Nelson's Wife	Mary Wilkes	5
To a Madame Bovary	Raymond Fenech	6
Death of a Vessel	Dorothy McFadyen	7
The Lost Artist	Bill Johnson	8
Thorn of a Rose	Joanna Ashwell	9
Rowan	Dylan Pugh	10
On Finding the Note by the Milkbottle	Paul Darby	11
No Chance to Say Goodbye	Pauline Hanson	12
Estrangement	Alwyn Trubshaw	13
Bad Timing	Doreen Baidoo	14
Untitled	John Rowland	15
Without Love	Teresa Webster	16
Delayed Burial	Jane Lee	17
I Used to Waken Singing	Gwen Hartland	18
A Teenage Tragedy	Alan Denne	19
Understanding the Stars	Alison Chisholm	20
Stay	Fiona Cork	21
Vampire	Colin R Loyns	22
Our Last Nightcap	Sally Eason	23
Cold Comfort	Katie Mallett	24
Dreams and Memories	Catriona Morrison	25
Drawing the Line	Gillian Capper	26
Off the Record	Marjorie Appleby	27
Guinevere	Alison Hall	28
Fall of the House of Windsor	Marguerite Corbett	29
Photograph	Mae Leonard	30
No More Talking	Paul Hampton	31
Not Over You	Ieuan Phillips	32
A Sensible Goodbye	Patricia Butterworth	33
You Closed the Door	Penny Witney	34

Title	Author	Page
Keep Trying	Peter Comaish	35
Does This Satisfy You?	Felicity Titley	36
Formal Warning	Judy Pavier Wilson	37
Inside Outside	Margaret Nicol	38
Traces	John Tirebuck	39
Rebirth of a Love Affair	Shirley Thompson	40
Deprivation	Mhairi J Jarvis	41
Rubble	Aspen	43
Without Words	Isabel Cortan	44
Is There an Answer	Brenda Benton	45
Say No More	Norman Harvey	46
The End of the Affair	Stephen Hunter	47
Gossip	Rosemary Bevan	48
I Loved You	A J Obrist	49
Adrift	Philip Williams	50
No More Words	Ann Das	51
Roundabouts	Margaret Paterson	52
Eyes Across the Room	Sheila Griffin	53
The Wedding	Hannah Little	54
Love Story	Alys Slater	55
The Last Stand	Ben Ingham	56
Glad I'm Not Dead	Carole Horsman	58
The Ebb And the Flow	Jim Wilson	59
One	Jane Thompson	60
The House of my Love	Frank Keetley	61
Separate Bed	Martin Holmes	62
Split	Shirley E Peckham	63
Tremors	David Whatley	64
Breaking up	Sue Williams	65
Days of Plenty	Dorothy Morris	66
The End	Andrew Collins	67
Parting in the Rain	Evelyn Foster	68
Cutout	Judd	70
Poor Little Sue	Doreen King	71
For the Love of Art	Pam Probert	72
The Parting	Dorothy Slaski	73
Decoy Duck?	Betty Lightfoot	74
Vacant Possession	Jan Porter	75

Title	Author	Page
The Betrayed Lover	Rochelle D Rabin	76
Centering	Alyson Faye	77
Barrabas Parting	Fletcher Cooper	78
The Quantocks - A Lovers' Quarrel	Norman Hurst	80
Freedom?	Dennis H Jackson	81
A Smooth Departure	Polly Heyes	82
Lament	Lee Sheldrake	83
Rebirth	B J Allen	84
Polite Promises	Tony Noon	85
Duet of Thoughts	Kathy Cox	86
Breaking up	Jan Free-Gore	87
Friend, you Must be Sad	Vincent M De Souza	88
The Tablecloth Trick	Nick Daws	89
Lover Mine, This is Our Love	Tobias Hill	90
Khayyam	Mal Jordan	91
A Silent Scream	Maureen Reynolds	92
Going Without	Dorothea Smartt	93
Assignation	Ilse Danby	94
Bereft	Hilary Tinsley	95
The Marriage Game	Lilian Parker	96
Ending it all	Philip Segar	97
Her Wreath	Shelagh Shannon	98
Full Time for us	David Wilkins	99
Break Point	Audrey Harbord	100
Regression	Carol Reynolds	101
Locked Within the Attic	Sue Gerrard	102
Middle and Both Ends	Jennifer Greenway	103
Lost	Shirley Silman	104
Solitude	Myk Jonson	105
Crisis	Divina McGonigal	106
When Death Comes Calling	M Finney	107
Seven Days of Love	Keely A Nethercott	109
Unsuccessful Attempt	Kevin Brewer	110
Like Distance	Philip J Faulkner	111
Alone Again	Jenny Prescott	112
Public Parting	Rosemary Rogan	113

Title	Author	Page
Confessions	Annette McFarline	114
I Talk to Myself	Francis Paul Farnworth	116
ice breaking	Malcolm Rayment	117
Overflow	Lorna Grinter	118
The Bitch	J W Nevill	119
The Promise	Shirley Boyson	120
Have a Guess	Ian J Blackman	121
Resuscitation	B C Godfrey	122
Untitled	Kevin James Moloney	123
Disbelief	Ian Shaw	124
On Adam's Retirement	Simeon Jebb	125
Loki	Nicole Brannan	126
A String of Pearls	A J McDonald	127
Water Into Wine	Graham Hitch	128
A Gardener	G M Albon	130
Broken Promises	Emma Shaw	131
A Letter from an Old Friend	Geoffrey Winch	132
The Eating of Britain	Brent Hodgson	134
The Braer	Chris Jones	135
Storm	Lucy Newsam	136
The Diamond Knife Tarnished	Suzanne Stratful	137
Swansong	Lesley Marshall	138
Match Point	Tom Miller	139
Fish on the Move	Julie Daly	140
Windswept	Nicola Plumb	141
Lover's Lament	Lynn Michelle Hiller	142
West Princes Street Gardens	Paul Berry	143
The Hour of Change	Laurie Carmen	144
Bridled And Broken In	Clementine Withy	145
Burnt Out	Peter Burns	146
The End of Love	Jill Dyer	147
Parliament Square	Angela Evans	148
The Torrent	Pat Jones	149
Stranded	Ingird Blanchard	150
Picking up the Pieces	Pattie Bancroft	151
The Little Old Lady of Bromley by Bow	Chris Porteous	153

Bitter Harvest	Flora M Cameron	154
This Time	Sally Angell	155
Brittle	Julia Lucie	156
Symbols	Deirdre van Outersterp	157
The Letters	Josie Boot	158
Untitled	Jane Fell	159
Songlines	Mary Smith	160
Shattering Illusions	Chris Davies	161
Birthday Card	James Adams	162
Independence Day	Vanessa Rivington	163
Got Away - Caught Again	Jock McGregor	164
Alone at Last	Hazel Jones	165
Experience	Stan Lee	166
Breaking Up	Gwynneth Curtis	167
I Lost my Love	Winifred Roberts	168
Passing Time	Clare Woods	169
The Signs The Hopes	Angela Gray	170
Subtle Hints of Demise	Chinedu	171
Letter to Sam	Mary Gilby	172
Exposé	June Heather Cook	173
Bitter Tears	Pollyanna	174
Void	Jennifer McDonald	175
Missing You	Malcolm Rayment	176
So Who's Deprived?	Eric Burke	177
Help - My Body Break Up Wanted - One Zip Fastener	Esther Hawkins	178
Loneliness	Jennifer Churches	179
The Rhythm of You	Zoe Dellous	180
End Game	Andy Gilbert	181
Act Too	Marlene Morris	182
Old Lovers	P M Holloway	183
Adder on the Stairs	John Nelson Holmes	184
Me and My Guy	Irene Giles	185
Too Little	Rahila Gupta	186
He Loves Me Not	Anne Butler	187
James	Ken Walmsley	188
Today I Discarded Part of My Life	Jeanne Brown	189

Title	Author	Page
The Fragile Frost	Barbara Jotham	190
Change of Form	Quibilah Montsho	191
Untitled	Derek Peter Ford	193
Late Summer	Sheila Parry	194
Alternate Weekends	Margaret Planeta	195
Waiting for the Wind	Barbara Moss	196
Walk Over Western Park	Sarah Wallace	197
Exit	Liz Yule	198
Lovers Quarrel	Arthur E Magnus	199
Sorry	Simon Kay	200
Midnight	Christopher Booth	201
A Prickly Relationship - Fading Fast	Adrian Jones	202
Lammas	Eamer O'Keeffe	203
Love in Mind	Brenda Dove	204
Susanna in Kaleidoscope	Robert Gregory Bishop	205
Once Again	V M Anne Jones	206
Untitled	Verena West	207
The Masochist	Denise Lee	208
Nightime Rain	Howard Atkinson	209
April Sixth and April Seventh	Lorreene Hunte	210
Sad Face	Tony Jones	211
Father's Day	Joan Bulmer	212
A Winter in My Heart	Mary Jones	213
Trinity	Greta Brickell	214
The Target	Pippa McCathie	215
Golden Web	Brian Covell	216
Cardiac Arrest	James Ahsman	217
A Vermilion Pool	Siân Headon	218
Normal Service Will be Resumed as Soon as Possible	Joy Adams	219
Lady Stopped Loving Me	Stuart Lancaster	220
Cain's Answer	Caole Carr	221
Breaking Up	Mary Hayworth	222
For He Who Waits	Ted Harrison	223
Wild Rose	Thomas M Ryder	224
Words	Margaret Sparvell	225

Already Naked	Chris Kenworthy	226
Recollection	Ane Stewart	227
Tampering	Don Smith	228
How Deep My Love	Collin West	229
Smileless	Kim Davies	230
Walls	Gladys M Green	231
Goodwill Message	Jennifer Holland	232
David's Plight	Peter Cranswick	233
Disappointment	Chinedu	234
Love's Victims	John Jolley	235

The Row

Like javelins at first
The words fly, light and lethal
To fell their prey.
They wound cleanly,
Propelled by the urgency of their quest,
And the white-hot hatred of their mission.
Then, as the first glorious rage subsides,
To be replaced by dull dislike,
Each syllable is dragged
From deeper down,
From ancient and compounded memories.
So this is the end of love:
A mindless slog across a mire of words.

Heather Smith

Jumped Upon

I ripped you apart like a curtain
or a cat with a rat
to shake you out of oblivion.
But you swallowed me up
cracked off the top of my head
and left me like a crushed eggshell.

Maureen Weldon

Window Gazing

Window gazing
Self effacing,
Rumbles of a distant past;
Leave of senses -
Sense of stealing!
Simply starved of love and last.

Rosalyn Carr

After the Masked Ball the Dirty Dancing

You were a woman
whose ways were a mask
your code of behaviour
a convention
an everyday task.
You saw me
as accoutrement
a public-worn mask
of self-adornment
and adoration
a situation in which
many girls bask
But today you tore away
your public-shown mask
and took what you wanted:
I saw the real you
stark in full lust.
I warmed to the task.
We both lost control.
Control too is a mask.

Our relationship now
is revealingly clear.
I know that in future
I won't have to ask.

Geoff Stevens

Nelson's Wife

Nelson married Fanny in a warm, southern clime
And brought her back to Burnham
In the bleak winter time.
      Cold through the keyhole
      Screamed the wind from the east;
      Straight across the marshes,
      Whipping man and beast.
Tearing at the windows, stealing under doors;
Fanny sighed and sickened for warm, southern shores.

Nelson went to battle and lost an arm and eye;
Fanny nursed him back to health
And would not let him die.
      Cold through the keyhole
      Roared the wind from the east,
      Straight across the marshes,
      Tiring man and beast.
Nelson met his Emma, Lady Hamilton;
Fanny was forgotten then; her day was done.

Emma kept both husband and lover by her side,
While Fanny nursed his father
Until the good man died.
      Cold through the keyhole
      Moaned the wind from the east,
      Straight across the marshes
      Chilling man and beast.
Summer came to Burnham, roses, scented, red;
Marshes bright with kingcups, but Nelson was dead.

Mary Wilkes

To a Madame Bovary

If it be blood
that runs through your veins
rivers are made of blood;

If it be a heart
that beats inside your chest
clocks are beating hearts;

If it be a human brain
that thinks inside your head
animals are better than humans;

If it be a conscience
that advises your actions
then conscience is a seducer;

If blood, heart, brain and conscience
are this much corrupt
there is no place for you,
on earth, in hell or in heaven!

Raymond Fenech

Death of a Vessel

Trapped . . .
within the eye of the storm,
Lashed by winds of fury,
buffeted by a fuming ocean
and crashing waves of destruction.

Gone the sea of tranquillity,
now a raging inferno,
a battle with the enemy of man,
a saboteur of life.

A vessel of majesty tossed like a cork,
splintered into fragments
and swallowed up like a venus flytrap
into the ocean graveyard.
The seas inhumanity to man,
just an echo from the phantom of the deep,
A cry for help unheard, unseen,
only the sound of the great 'Amen'

Dorothy McFadyen

The Lost Artist

We named him, gently mocking, Rembrandt.
In truth Douanier Rousseau would have been
Nearer the mark, but too pretentious.
He was a fair weather man
Who never painted in the rain
Which soaked his studio, a wide grass verge.
But all of summer, and fine winter days
He came by bicycle - Rousseau again? -
And parked, and talked to idle passers-by
Or, beret squarely set, faced the farm house
And painted a white horse.
People living miles away would say
'I can't remember where you live -
The village name - I know it as the one
Where that old artist sits'. Like us
They did not ask his name.
And now, is it too late?
He was not here on Christmas Day
Nor any day since then
And now is summer in, the grass
Deep on his studio floor.
We give up waiting, finding nothing
But the ultimate reason, and resent
With bitterness this brash intrusion.
Death should have other things to do
Than interfere in such an innocent affair.

Bill Johnson

Thorn of a Rose

Blood from her finger flows like a stream from a hill.
Tears in her eyes run so freely yet still.
Stained lace on the ground,
the only symbol to be left.

One gift of love,
now gives her such pain.
Light fades from her world.
Tears of the angels rain down.

Weeping for her heartache,
she's saturated through to her soul.

His footsteps are felt like tossing stones
on top of his heart.
The knowledge of his mistake,
he'll carry like a thorn.

His own heart will be torn,
cut to the stem with her own.
Each will blossom again,
lovers tainted by the thorn of a rose.

Joanna Ashwell

Rowan

You planted me a rowan,
For once I told you how I loved
Their flush of autumn leaves,
The bloody drops of scarlet fruit.

You never could accept
My Grandam's tales; how things of evil
Would not venture near
A house protected by the mountain ash.

I never really knew myself
Whether I could believe.
But since you left me here
This house has had a haunting every day.

Dylan Pugh

On Finding the Note by the Milkbottle

just a scrap of paper
ragged edges;
it was the discovery that shocked you.
locked, bewildered glances
bring thoughts of yesterday's unwashed plates,
two coffee cups cold.
you mouth the harshly scribbled words
slowly
one by one
finally realising
he is gone:

one word bites hard
sorry love.

Paul Darby

No Chance to Say Goodbye

('Our hopes for the future
have faded away,
But memories will always stay.')

I heard the knock upon the door and knew,
Before I even saw him, why he'd come;
A sunny August morning, clouds were few . . .
And yet my flesh was ice . . . my feelings numb;
He didn't need to speak; moist eyes said all.
'What time?' I asked. 'Six-thirty,' he replied.
'Did he wake up?'
      'He sighed and seemed to call
Your name, my mother said, . . . and then he died.'

You 'passed on peacefully,' they all acclaimed;
And yet, how could they know? Perhaps you fought
From deep within your coma and exclaimed;
Reluctant, loathe to leave, perhaps you thought
Like me, it was unfair that you should die
So young.
      We had no chance to say Goodbye!

Pauline Hanson

Estrangement

This end was in the beginning.
    First the words, the knife,
    death of my life.
    Then the smile, balm
    that brought no calm.
    Then acrid taste
    of discontent;
    bleak arid waste
    of banishment;
    desires born
    to be frustrate;
    anger, scorn,
    fierce flash of hate;
    spirit hammering to escape
    futile venomous debate . . .
    festered lily or sour grape?

I am shot through with arrows of the dark.
    They throng and thud
    finding their mark,
    and poison spread
    in my heart's blood . . .
    How shall I be comforted?

This end was in the beginning.
    though now it ache
    heart shall not break,
    yet now is no relief
save by this salve of utterance
    for my grief
until these rabid onslaughts cease
and to a mind inflamed annealing time
brings frozen peace

Alwyn Trubshaw

Bad Timing

Insults, crashing, screaming, fighting,
Punching, kicking, scratching, biting,
Silence, crying, heaving, sighing.
On the bed he finds her lying -
He looks.

Looking, talking, getting nearer.
Watching, listening, speaking clearer.
Silence, touching, heaving, sighing.
On the floor they both are lying -
He loves.

Loving, needing, feeling weaker.
Wanting, fearing feeling meeker.
Silence, holding, feeling smaller.
What can he do to feel taller -
He hates.

Hating loving, insults flying,
Hating wanting, punches flying,
Hating fearing, crashes, lying.
On the bed he finds her dying -
He cries.

Crying, silence, heaving, sighing,
On the bed he finds her dying.
Crying, silence, heaving, sighing,
On the floor they both are lying -
He cries -
She dies.

Doreen Baidoo

Untitled

'My eyes, my eyes - with the mist it's hard to see'

The mist winds in from the sea,
thick with winding sheets and
navigated sarcophagi, the dead
ocean mists of scientific dreams,
panegyrics, a million careless dead
things caressing their deadweed stones,
colder than the breath of forgotten gods.

I loved you to your soul -
soul love - now that love
is lost

And all the death-pale things
on the beach mark a change in the weather
on the scree, the scream of the screaming stones.

John Rowland

Without Love

Here in the dark
 alone with silence
waves mock me
 sometimes I think I
hear ripple on shore
 sand untrodden curves
towards horizon
 to unknown unquiet ocean

Darkness covers me
 through window dark tree
limbs whisper secrets
 into night. I am alone
here on the edge of silence
 half afraid, waiting a sign

In my heart
 tides set motion
a light from cloudless
 moon touches me
I can hear sea
 laughing along sand
I must turn again
 Silence beckons me
once more I sleep.

Teresa Webster

Delayed Burial

We've agreed to bury this farce
And each take our separate ways,
Accepting an equal proportion of blame
While planning the coming days;
We've displayed great depth of control,
Not voicing abuse or complaint,
Dividing the trappings of all the good years
With commendable restraint.

Why, then, should I weep in the dark
Aware of your grief through the wall,
Or startle upright from my own anguished sleep
To answer your dream - thick call?
The clear-cut decisions of day
By night become tearstained and blurred -
Oh why must it take such a torturous time
For the corpse to be interred?

Jane Lee

I Used to Waken Singing

I used to waken singing.

My mood now blue-black as a raven's wing,
With images splattered on my mind's eye
Like ink islands from the meandering
Of a palsied hand. A murmur . . . My sigh?
Or is it night talk of garden creatures?
I peer into a water-lily pond.
Ripples travel on reflected features,
Splitting their being. Sending them beyond
Reality. Beyond interest now
To me, drowned in the noxious pool: despair.
A cloud sheds tears and darkens the moon's brow.
Or are they my tears for a dead affair?

I used to waken singing.

Gwen Hartland

A Teenage Tragedy

My life is over, in ruins, the pits
My girlfriend just dumped me for another boy
I can't think straight, I'm at the end of my wits
Because of my love for a girl called Joy
She told me we were like Romeo and Juliet
And that our love would be everlasting
My yearnings so I haven't eaten yet
I wonder if Mum's noticed I'm fasting?

It's been a week to the day since she said we're through
And I've taken to eating to comfort my sorrow
I doubt if she'd still love me with this extra pound or two
So it's down to the diet first thing tomorrow
The spots have begun to appear round my face
My skin's turned grey and my eyes have sunk
The mirror shows someone else in my place
Pity I'm too young to go out and get drunk!

I've survived two weeks of heartache now
My appetite left with my urge to die
She never even phoned, the selfish cow
Probably too wrapped up in her hunky new guy
While I'm upset, she's having fun
Maybe it's time to do the same
There's a new girl next door and I've got to run
Oh well! I guess I'm over what's-her-name!

Alan Denne

Understanding the Stars

I did not close my eyes the night you left.
I lay alone and still, watched evening sky
disgorge its hidden cache of jewels. The cleft
between us was as deep, the wall as high
as space dividing star from empty star.
It seemed each pin prick held a secret hoard
of colours unperceived before, and far
and farther ranged the frequencies, a sword
to slash the spectrum, severing each thread
that linked my mind to reason. Learning pain
I reached to touch the dark side of my bed.
Shock of its chill exploded in my brain.
  New colours flared and died; despairing grew.
  No universe can take the place of you.

Alison Chisholm

Stay

If I could keep you with me
by sowing seeds of need
deep inside you,
I would do it.

If I could use my breath to
fill your lungs and my
blood to line your veins,
I would do it.

I want to weld you to me,
fuse your legs with mine
to stop you walking
without me.

Fiona Cork

Vampire

My strength is almost gone now;
The fight that I once had has left,
Eroded by my unanswered letters,
Ebbing away as my calls are unreturned.
I feel you slipping away my love,
My fingers lack the will to grasp your hand;
I am letting you go, watching you drift away
To save myself from this downward spiral.

As I watch you float away,
I can see pieces of myself next to you;
My self confidence, my passion for life,
My energy. Two years of memories
Are just souvenirs for your mantelpiece,
Trinkets for you to place with the photographs
And that tacky statuette from the Greek Islands.
You fade into the sunset, I slip into the night.
I'm just too tired to fight.

Colin R Loyns

Our Last Nightcap

raised voices
we recognise
this won't end nicely:
retreat
sleep
and feel distant in the morning.

Sally Eason

Cold Comfort

Unable to believe the words you wrote
I took your letter with me
To read again in the park.

My eyes brimmed full as the sullen lake
As your meaning sank into me,
Like the deadly teeth of a shark.

On the way home I had to shop.
I dreamt that you were with me,
Filled my bag with apple tart.

And ice-cream that we wouldn't share.
Your letter lay with my shopping,
As frozen as my heart.

Katie Mallett

Dreams and Memories

Gone
But for my dreams

Never
But in my hopes

Lost
But for my memories

Without
But for my heart.

Catriona Morrison

Drawing the Line

I love your lacerating wit,
Your vicious, blatant lies.
I love your desperation
And the terror in your eyes.
I love the way you look at me
As if I wasn't there.
I even love the way you tell me that you do not care.
I love you, love you, love you, dear, exactly as you are
But even for a masochist like me
You go too far.

Gillian Capper

Off the Record

He came to me all scented from the wood.
And wooed me with his jewelled eyes and honeyed tongue of love.
I lifted up my eyes and watched the apple fall,
Wondering why I'd not thought of it myself.
      Then spoke that slimy slippery ape,
       'Twas the woman tempted me.
       T'was her mistake.'
This side of Eden, let me put the record straight,
It wasn't Adam or the fruit I fancied
Just the snake!

Marjorie Appleby

Guinevere

A modern-day maelstrom
In an urban dark,
Looking down on yellow haze,
The tops of street lights, clashing
Headlamps, 'Avalon' thrown unread
On the floor, too close
For comfort.

Tired of looking down at the endless
Flow and ebb of urgency into the city,
She turned to catch her image
In the mirror, sideways on, in blue,
And a voice echoed distantly
'You look like Guinevere in that dress'.

A staccato of light on the window,
A car, not passing this time, arriving,
A key in the door below.
She looked down again, to where the traffic dashed,
Headlights throwing gleaming fingers of accusation
Into the darkness.

Alison Hall

Fall of the House of Windsor

The monarchy once sat
triumphant in their Ivory Tower.
Above reproach
And beyond our power.
Surrounded by treasures
Naught but the richest ever saw.

Cocooned from the blows
Safe in a tax haven,
Revered and resplendent.

But now the house of cards falls
and they are repentant.

So now coldness and clarity prevail,
and gross imperfections are frail,
And mystic legends of years
have failed.

The burning of the castle
is of no avail.

Marriages
relationships,
The illusion is frail,
At the fall of The House of Windsor.

The image of perfection crumbles,
Popularity wanes and stumbles,
And the crystallised tower
shatters and fades,

As they no longer continue
to play charades.

Marguerite Corbett

Photograph

Depending on the light
and the time of year
the sun sometimes glints
the red in your hair
and you are there, really.

I hear you chuckle
the way you used to
knowing what I had to say
before the words formed
on my lips.

But nobody, not even you
could have predicted
this is where we are now
oceans between us
after all the rainy days.

When the snow came
in avalanche proportions
it cut off the narrow pass
and neither of us
could clear a path

I smile at you there
standing on the sideboard
talk to you, firmly believing
in telepathy. It is one
of the tricks for my survival

willing you back home.

Mae Leonard

No More Talking

You come, beneath the yews,
With priest before to cry
Your soul away;
You ride, alone, the mists and dews
Of grey oblivion.

You steal, all rules obeyed,
Into the church's gloom,
And leave your name;
The last, perhaps, in slow parade,
There's room or time for now.

We'll go, by fear oppressed,
On floods of dying
(No gatherings, no tears,
To show how good we were, or blessed,
Over the years -
Only the Great Storm, sighing).
We shall go thousands down,
Clutching at life and breath,
Into the chaos grown
From greed. We shall go sick to death -
Still love defying.

There will be firmaments -
Sun's light, and star's ;
Silence at last,
And no more talking.

Paul Hampton

Not Over You

I remember you as a sparkling, wild-eyed beauty
I gazed at a picture in my mind.
And lost myself in who I thought you were.

I remember you as a laughing, soaring, graceful spirit,
And wondered how you could address me
In tones so pure and not stooping.

I remember your eyes deep with contradiction and sadness
And loved you for it because I knew
You were like me.

I remember we kissed
And thought I was scorched by the fire of innocent passion.
I wish we had lingered longer there.

One day I hope I will value your friendship
And I know I will lay down your ghost
Until I do, she walks with me and is silent.

And I am not over you.

Ieuan Phillips

A Sensible Goodbye

You know
how much we loved each other
once,
and so do I:
but let's not beat about the bush -
we've had too many differences
lately . . .
no longer see eye to eye.

We know
the signals are set at danger
now,
you and I -
can feel the last clash coming:
so let's face it squarely
and try
to say a sensible goodbye.

Thinking back,
we excelled as sparring partners
from the start,
didn't we?
Untroubled love was not our angle,
yet sparks of love lit every tangle
of wit and will.
I'll miss their overspill,

wont you?

Patricia Butterworth

You Closed the Door

Softly, very softly
You closed the door
And shut me out
Of your world of fresh mountains
Deep lakes
And scarce-trodden grass.
Your voice comes to me, muffled
As you look about you
And tell me all you see.
What good is that to me?
My side of the door
Is beige, matt,
A soft grey carpet holds my feet.
A clock ticks on. The phone rings.
Your voice far off
Describes breadth and depth.
I see walls.
Open the door,
Invite me out
Please
I need the light,
The bright
Sharp sight
Of green and blue
And distant hue
And you.

Penny Witney

Keep Trying

Why do you pack your seething
your loathing and your hate
between your eyes like time bombs?
Don't sit around and wait
for news of the disaster
to smack you with the glare
of lurid, lazy, lounging
that kills the will to dare.

He who beats the cancer
that has ground his neighbour up
when the host puts hope on offer
will not throw away the cup.
For success has never frightened him
and failure's well defined:
as the prison where a trier
finds the snare to snag his mind.

Peter Comaish

Does This Satisfy You?

When I showed you
the joyous love poem
I was sending in for the competition,
you said, shocked,
'Couldn't you find something less personal?'
(something less pornographic, I think you meant)
So I wrote you and me out;
I took away
the vital, pulsating, throbbing
thing that was you
and the softly surging, gently welcoming
thing that was me
and saw
that what was left
were stark white bones,
a skeleton:
so, I sent in, instead,
a requiem for our relationship.

Felicity Titley

Formal Warning

Warning to a soldier who fails to measure up to army standards . . .
    Was it at the first meeting
    Or perhaps the second
    That I surrendered to a chemical attack?
    Anyway I recall the onslaught of desire
    As you lay siege to me.

It has been brought to my attention
That you have admitted to an extra marital association . . .
    September and the canal was ours
    We were alone with its glassy discretion,
    Rapt in those fragrant paths,
    Smothered in foliage, silenced by mud,
    The camouflage of my heart was wearing thin.

This deplorable behaviour and irresponsible attitude
reveals a total lack of integrity which must raise considerable doubts
about your fitness to retain SNCO rank.
You are formally warned that conduct of this nature
by a member of the armed services will not be tolerated . . .
    In the sweet warfare of our embraces
    The chained bullet around your neck
    Rang like a warning.
    I bolted from my fox-hole
    Under enemy fire.

In the meantime the immediate effects of this warning are as follows:
Screening from movement, a bar to advancement in rank,
The possibility of discharge, reduction or re-mustering.
    Employing few tactical manoeuvres,
    You discharged me from your heart.
    I was reduced to mustering
    All of my strength against the withdrawal
    Of your forces.

Judy Pavier Wilson

Inside Outside

Back down?
Apologise?
To see you humble
Will be a surprise.

Down town
You treated me badly;
Knocked me about
So I'll go gladly.

Safe now,
From your fists.
I may be your wife
But I don't deserve this.

Black-eyed,
I won't take you back.
Get Out!
Don't give me flack.

Swear then.
You have an ugly side.
You've lost me.
Now I'll hurt inside,
Not outside.

Margaret Nicol

Traces

There is evidence of blood here.
Ask yourself why.
A finger has been pricked,
There was broken glass,
Slivers linger yet,
Traces of a domestic scene,
Presupposing voices raised,
No, maybe only one.
We cannot say with certainty.
Violence, yes,
Then likely some remorse,
Or else, where is the glass?
The picture of a loved one or a place,
A shattered frame, a desecrated face.
Gone, too severely damaged
To ever be restored.
Would analysis reveal the salt of tears?
Are there traces of a trauma captured here?
You must decide.
Do you feel the ghosts of sad despair,
Or, 'Hold me very tight,'
And reconciliation in the air?

John Tirebuck

Rebirth of a Love Affair

When love dies,
What is left?
A flame expires, it
Goes out, of life
With it a heart
Grows cold,
Hope dies and
Dreams perish.

When love returns,
All is found.
The flame, rekindled,
Grows again, into
A passion, all consuming.
And is warm,
Hope flourishes, and
Dreams are reborn.

Shirley Thompson

Deprivation
(caused by break up)

To my absentee father -

Parent, who never knew me,,
you are but an image to me.

You chose not to show up
to watch me grow up.

Now, saying this may not seem fine,
but - the loss was yours more than it was mine,
and,

it's too late ever to know you.
It was my fate never to show you
what it would have meant to me
to have been a credit to you.

At least, I'm not indebted to you
for love - kept well hidden from me.

If you had shown more civility,
I might have known more tranquillity,
by being made aware that you did care for me.

It would have given me security
if you had given me the surety,
of, being aware that you would be there for me.

I missed your presence many days.
I inherited your many ways,
but, that is little consolation to me.

I could have loved you, but, I will never show you -
it was not my fate.
I would have loved you, but, I will never know you -
it is too many years too late.

from the 'result' - your stranger daughter.

Mhairi J Jarvis

Rubble

I am screaming
out another false birth
stretching the scars
which constrict my heart
as I dig graves for
my irrelevant feelings.

Memory shines as
a crafty draught
sneaks barefaced
into our aching bed.
How many more changes
must I go through?

Spirit journeys
steal the mind
as festering life
unfolds the new wings
of more strange creatures
to inhabit the soul.

Disappointment
is such a sodden
fresh chilled being
dripping raw through
twisted thoughts into
cracks of feeling.

Aspen

Without Words

a savage sound
sharp crack of a man's hand
across a woman's chin.

a ritual sound
her weeping in the dark
burying her love.

Isabel Cortan

Is There an Answer

Despair has really set in,
they begin to hate each other.
Husband off out with the boys,
wife, tied up as a mother.

With no olive branch on offer
things seem to be out of hand.
But this is not the full story,
it is not what God has planned.

For He is the Mighty Healer,
there's no marriage He can't mend.
By opening up their lives to Him
they'll find He is their friend.

He'll take every situation
and show them what to do.
If He's head of their household
they'll know a love that's true.

Hurt and misunderstandings
will then be washed away.
And united in their worship
they begin to pray each day.

Brenda Benton

Say No More

Say no more:
no further wounding words to lacerate
the thousand cuts of softly spoken
denigration.
If only you had raved your rancour,
but your voice as gentle as a dove,
like a dying fall
has said it all.
What I had thought in innocence was love
clothed a closet detestation.

Say no more:
no lisping honeyed words that once you spoke,
nor these the pent-up fury of masked
malignity.
But why dissemble? Why simulate
that which clearly you have never felt
except to mock me
designedly?
When I remember how this heart would melt
assuming fond fidelity.

Silent now,
you hang your head; is it penitence?
But contrition now this love will not
again restore.
I gaze upon these nerveless fingers,
wonder-eyed, that they have silenced lips
softly venomous,
if passionless.
And in the drumming of my ears is heard
the silence where you'll say no more.

Norman Harvey

The End of the Affair

The end, so long deferred and dreaded
Came as she had half expected
Like scene from film or book
But devoid of glamour. One look
At the note on the barren dresser
Enough to panic planets into wild ellipses.
The shadow of a double-decker bus
Across the bitter unmade bed. Outside
Customary bedlam of horns and motors.

She trod the streets, mechanical daze
In shopping malls and sheltered ways
It seemed the unremitting gaze
Of a cold world scything through her.
'Through drawn-out nights and empty days
This pall of darkness sits and stays
My grief descends in greater force
If only it would run it's course
Or let me drown in anger.'

On a buried afternoon she reached
Brent's shallow waters, rubble-beached
Within the sight of Wembley's towers;
Wembley's twin towers, domed and white.
'Not deep enough for suicide. I'll swim or sink
On life's raw tide. I know he's gone forever.'
She brushed a tear, then clenched a fist
'Dear God, that things could come to this!
Sometimes I think I've had enough
Of life and love and all that stuff.'
She bowed her head. 'Almost enough
Of life and love, and all that stuff.'

Stephen Hunter

Gossip

There'll be no more twitching curtains
at number twenty-four.
Disappointed voyeurs since
I won't see you any more.

No more gossip over loose meat
in the supermarket queue
discussing dreadful, wicked things
they just know I did to you.

Their lives will have no meaning
when they're sitting in the park
no more dreams and stories
of what we did when it grew dark.

Our passion spread like ripples
and coursed through their old blood
Their sexual life-support switched off
now that you're gone for good.

Rosemary Bevan

I Loved You

I loved you
But that was not enough
You had to have all
To make up for your insufficiency.

I was successful and brought all to you
For us to enjoy together
Mine and yours
But you could not forgive my success.

I gave you a son and stayed home
To look after him
Stayed home and worked at your interests
But it was not enough for you.

Your insecurity, your fear
Took you to drink. From drink to abuse.
From abuse to violence.
Yet I loved you still.

You were the taskmaster for our son.
Nothing could be right.
You undermined him with your own insecurity.
Yet it was not enough.

Until when he feared you and loathed you,
And I could take no more

And we left

You harassed and pursued us with your own self hate,
Your own self fear, your own insecurity
Your power to hate and destroy those whom loved you most.

A J Obrist

Adrift

While strolling by the sea,
In happy mood or blue,
I often long to see,
A girl that once I knew.
That resolved will tumble,
Wither through the night,
Resolutions all crumble
When love is still alight.
Boats have finished burning,
Now I am all adrift,
A wild persistent yearning,
Says - time to heal the rift.

Philip Williams

No More Words

Oh! How we used to talk
About everything under the sun -
With each topic exhausted
Another would come.

Today we look abstractly -
Today we sit and stare.
Even if we wanted them,
No more words are there.

Ann Das

Roundabouts

I lie still in the dark of the night
You are already asleep
Breathing deeply, dreaming of her
She who helps you prove your manhood
It's my choice you say
Whether you stay close to me
Sharing the marital bed
Providing the occasional touch
Of your hard unloving mouth
Or you leave with your latest passion
The white flesh of your bare arm
Covers my naked body
No longer the cause of your lust
Am I just the nearest person to hold
As you dream of youth and softer skin
You can't give her up you say
And I can't live alone
My life is too big for one
You have left me nothing to give
For I have given you my all
I have no love for anyone else
You stole and spent all my emotions
Spent them on swings and roundabouts
So we'll carry on living our lives
And I'll be waiting here patiently for you
Comforted by thoughts of yesterday's love
Beyond these memories
I expect and need nothing more
But your return.

Margaret Paterson

Eyes Across the Room

Eyes across the room; has it been like this before?
Difficult to concentrate as small talk becomes a bore.
Knowing he's moving slowly through noisy crowds to me,
Wondering what he'll say, and how different things will be.
Now he's reached my side; sweet anticipation flares.
Words come easily to us; but his nearness rips and tears
A path of pain right through me, and I know that there will be
Much sadness in our loving, too early yet to see.

Eyes across the room have become hand enclosed in hand;
An urge to be together, to pick up every strand
Of eager conversation, and so entwine our minds,
That we both must keep on searching and delight in golden finds
What brings soulmates together? How can two blend as one?
To share sweet joys of living in rain and wind and sun.
So now we have escaped there is no sense or rhyme,
Only ecstasy that lifts us up and out of time.

Eyes across the room have become sweet fulfilment of love
A blend of passion and peace, raging lion and gentle dove.
There is much to do and to see; I knew our time would be brief
Inner warnings become more urgent, such happiness must bring grief.
We seem to have shared a lifetime, so now that he has to go,
The child that our love created will one day grow to know
That the time I spent with his father enriched me for all my life.
Whatever the world cares to do to me now, for one year I was his wife.

Sheila Griffin

The Wedding

It was thirty summers ago
That we swore undying devotion,
Faithful till death do us part,
Filled with burning emotion.

It was seventeen summers ago
That you went away without warning,
'Don't cry for too long' you said,
As you left with your bag in the morning.

It was thirteen summers ago
That you blithely went to your wedding,
Joined yourself to another,
Left me, a widow in mourning.

Now, as we stand here together,
Our daughter radiant in white,
Making the same vows that we made,
In both their eyes the same light;

What do you feel as we stand here?
Does your heart pray the same prayer as mine?
That for them there will be no undoing,
That their love will last for all time.

Or is there, for you, a moment,
A moment suspended in time,
Confronted by guilt and concupiscence,
The Judgement, in a moment of time.

But the moment has passed, now;
Vengeance is Mine, says the Lord . . .
It's time to witness the signing,
Time to forget what you heard.

Hannah Little

Love Story

We were one body;
together in a crowded room
our conversation held
the warmth of touching;
later, in the act of love
we poured our own libations,
wove cords of passion,
wrote endless futures.

We are now parted;
a silent bleeding leaves
these shadows underneath my eyes;
you are a hostile stranger
sealed against all touching
so I deny eternity,
the agony between us,
the wounded future.

Alys Slater

The Last Stand

I cannot carry on
Loving on a knife's edge.
Pretty soon sadness will fall,
I will get cut
And bare the scars,
Like a mad axeman
Amidst chic ladies
With cigarette holders;
I inhale the perfume
And spend the night
In your hotel room.

I thought once,
But I was wrong
As I drove into the sunset,
That I could see you
In the corner of my eye,
You looked sad,
As though somehow
Your heart was broken.
Did you hear me pining?
I was waiting by the telephone;
I was scared
Of spending the night
On my own.
You said you wanted me
So now I need to know.

You were standing there
Alone in the shadows
With a gun . . .
It was pointing at me;
Somehow I knew
That this was it.
I was hit, hurt,
My heart was bleeding,
Cut to the quick
And screaming in agony,
Writhing in pain
As you walked away from me.

Ben Ingham

Glad I'm Not Dead

'You don't understand,' I sobbed to my mum.
'My heart has been broken and you're making fun.'
'You're fourteen,' said my mum, 'with a whole life ahead.'
'You're wrong,' I screamed back, 'I wish I were dead.'
'Listen,' snapped mum, 'you're being a pain
Using that same old story again.
Last week it was Ian, before that it was Jay,
And you said you quite fancied Pete yesterday.'
'Oh God, she's unbearable,' mum said to dad,
'Adam just dumped her, she's driving me mad.
Crying and whinging and not eating her food
I can't even talk to her in this sort of mood.'
I ran upstairs to be on my own,
That's when I heard the ring of our phone.
Mum called me down. 'It's for you dear,' she said;
It turned out to be Pete and I'm glad I'm not dead.
'Reprieved,' smiled my mum as I accepted the date,
'This is it,' I grinned back, 'it has to be fate.'
Adam can take a hike from now on,
My heart lies with Pete where it belongs.

Carole Horsman

The Ebb And the Flow

As I lie here all night long,
My thoughts turn to where love has gone,
Those early days of tranquillity,
Wondering where they were leading me.

Feelings of love within my being,
A kindred spirit we were seeing,
Our children we brought to life,
In those early days we felt no strife.

As those tides of passion turned,
Angry words and emotions burned,
Who's fault it was I'll never know,
Seeds of doubt they bloom and grow.

Many times I've walked those trails,
How could we go off the rails
That sorrow in our young one's eyes,
A billion tears I have cried.

The innocent should bear no blame,
Their young lives can't be the same,
Pain never stopped for me and you,
There's Granma's Grandad's and family too.

Through those lonely passing years,
I often wonder why,
Through these misty running tears
I searched both sea and sky.

I am much older and wiser now,
With understanding to help me through,
So when new buds break upon the bough,
Brings memories of our young love so true.

Jim Wilson

One

The empty bottle,
Placed on the step,
A reminder that once,
Not so long ago,
There were two.

Try to shut the door,
On its malicious form,
Reject the image from my mind,
Pretend it has no relevance,
To my new found situation.

A clatter startles the silence,
Prompting mirthless laughter,
The lone vessel lies shattered
Spiky shards glinting,
Resolutely, I pick up the pieces.

Jane Thompson

The House of my Love

The day that the house of my love fell down
It took such little blows;
No huff
Or puff
Not even full-blown gale;
But just the gentle breezes
Born of love's neglect.
Of lack of compliments' pointing
To save the soft cement,
Or panes of a heart's windows
Lost for touch up paint.
Foundations undermined
By jealous hidden streams
Eroding the soft sands
On which our hope was based.
Neglect of care and maintenance,
Sinful lack of thought;
Symptoms of the weaknesses
From which defeat was bought.

Frank Keetley

Separate Bed

We kept the double bed
We didn't go for singles.
We kept the double bed
It's double, but separate.
When it's all made up
It looks just fine
It's only when we slip inside,
That an ice cold, invisible
Insurmountable line, slowly
Appears down the middle
To divide your side
From mine.

Martin Holmes

Split

Breaking up
over showers of tears
amidst armies of fears.

No time for cheers.

Two split dears
in a jamming of gears
after harmonious years.

Shirley E Peckham

Tremors

As love sends tremors to the heart
So does the earth. Catastrophes
That cable from across the world
Collect in living rooms. O television,
My anaesthetist - you dull disaster.
Like unrequited love, we pray
It happens somewhere else. Forget.

But more about these tremors of the heart:
That seldom-watered rose has slumped,
And if the vase is chipped then chuck it out.
Sweet nothings grow on trees these days,
Incarnate flower and fruit. Uproot.

And should you languish in a loft
Remember this: most solitude is brief.
The moon will be your neutral analyst -
she listens with a less discerning ear -
Attics of half-lit lust, a lingering
Of love. Again, begin, again.

And will beginnings end? I think they must.
Such tremors televisions won't report.
Unlike the tanks at Tiananman
This tragedy will happen to us all,
Its havoc harnessed to
An uninvited epitaph: we failed at love.

David Whatley

Breaking up

He said that he loved me
Did he not?
He must have changed his mind somehow,
And quickly - forgot.

He said he'd give me everything,
Even a ring.
But somehow he went off, somewhere else,
And didn't say a thing.

He wrote a note explaining
Just how bad he felt.
Oh wait for me, 'my darling',
And in my arms - you'll melt.

But, I don't think I will bother.
No, he's not the one for me.
How dare he call me, 'Darling',
And use me, - so callously.

Sue Williams

Days of Plenty

Do you remember
The golden leaves
In the orchard?
The damsons, purple and thick
Upon the tree?
The apples,
That we gave to one and all,
Plums, such plums!
And Williams pears,
And that snuffling hedgehog
That we tried to tame,
Do you remember
the Autumn,
Before the Winter came?

Dorothy Morris

The End

The miracle of love has gone,
And so we leave the summit we climb,
And part with our last kiss.
The past was pure and happy with so
Much to share,
But we grow older in our time,
To realise we were really strangers,
So in the end we walk hand in hand,
And part where our hearts found us.

Andrew Collins

Parting in the Rain

We sit
Hand in hand
In the rain
Of my departure;
Weighed down
And awash
With grief.
The water falls
Relentlessly
Bruising our cheeks
With raindrops.

Raindrops
Only raindrops
But later
When the rain stops
Will they prove
To be tear drops
On your face
As on mine?

I remember once
When I laid my heart bare
Your taking my hair
In your hand;
As if reluctant,
Even so briefly
Ever to quite let me go.

Yet now
As the rain
Drops
(Will the rain
Ever stop?)
I am leaving
And you have let
Go.

You
Binding me to being
With a chain made of maybes
Forged of lost unheeded hopes -
The fantasies of fools.

After all
Only fools sit out
In the rain

Or hold on to hair
As to hope.

Only fools . . .

And lovers.

Evelyn Foster

Cutout

Inside I tear easily.
Your look is weapon enough.
Indifference wields a sharper blade
and you know how to use it.

Judd

Poor Little Sue

I went to the bar to have a gin and tonic.
How was I to know she was really fond of it?
We sat down side by side and had a drink or two,
And then she told me that her name was little Sue.
She was wearing one of those black low-necked dresses.
What she had underneath didn't take many guesses.
I took her out and we wined and dined together.
And I thought that she was really pretty clever.
I gave her a little champagne and caviar,
And then we had a few more drinks at the bar.
I pay for what I want and as I paid for it
I felt that now I certainly deserved a bit,
So I asked my chauffeur to drive us to my door,
And I took her all the way up to the top floor.
We spent the whole night on my sheepskins and leathers,
And she submitted freely to my endeavours.
Then, early in the morning, I sent her packing,
And she said that my manners were rather lacking.
How on earth was I to know she would get pregnant?
And so just barely sufficient money was sent.
I can't have my name mentioned anywhere at all.
I'm not to blame as I always play it so cool.
Anyway it's nothing at all to do with me.
The baby's her problem as it will always be.
I pay the price for what I want and always do,
So no more will be said about poor little Sue.

Doreen King

For the Love of Art

If I could have painted a picture of our love,
It would have been the soft glowing pink
and tender white of a dove.
If I could have painted the emotion
that I felt for you,
It would have been green and gold,
and deep azure blue.
If I could have captured the light
that shone from your eyes,
It would have been like soft golden sunlight,
the colour of rain washed skies.
If I could have painted the spark
when your lips touched mine,
It would have been electric blue
and silver . . . brilliantly sublime.
You had coloured my life with a beautiful hue,
But now you're gone,
She has you instead!
My palette is black,
The artist is dead.

Pam Probert

The Parting

Perhaps with time we'll see things clearly and understand it all,
this sorry state we've come to, cases packed and in the hall.
God knows we tried, time and again, to bring back what we'd lost.
I'd changed, you had too, and now we count the cost,
of words said carelessly perhaps, but none the less preventing,
this fragile thing that was our love from actually cementing.

The bitterness that crept in and caught us when off guard,
all too soon became a habit, it really wasn't hard.
So much time was spent in pointless recriminations,
and never quite enough, it seems, in tender ministrations.
We used to laugh a lot and love each other madly,
But now we know it's over and regret that its ended badly.

Thank goodness we're not married, the way ahead is clear,
to separate with dignity and scarcely shed a tear.
So goodbye my erstwhile lover, I'll remember you with affection,
I hope you wont forget me as we step in a new direction.
Always remember the joy we had and look towards tomorrow.
I'll do the same and maybe soon, I'll cast away this sorrow.

Dorothy Slaski

Decoy Duck?

Discovered, upside down in loo
Bathtime Duck all limp and blue
Message inside bowl said this:
'Had my fill of Married Bliss'
As Bimbo flushes truth from sight
Husband stabs her with sharp knife . . .

Betty Lightfoot

Vacant Possession

Long before I left,
the rooms were changed.
Cold, mocking ritual -
the glasses brimming,
tables laid.
Across familiar surfaces,
we kept colliding - out of sync.
Doubt, imperceptible as dust,
webbed every corner of our lives.

Now
as I watch you move away,
desert the deep, disturbing echoes of this house -
it is the final letting-go that hurts,
prickling of old scars I thought long healed.

In restless dreams I search the garden path.
Loiter near the pool.
Open our bedroom window -
shadowy pass through
       to where the paintings blaze with colour.
       Vases chant out loud again
       a symphony of Summer flowers . . .

Yet I do not, cannot blame you.
Won't fritter time on bitterness, regret.
Inexorably,
your freedom is my freedom, too.
Together or apart - the Past belies us.
Future's for the building up,
setting down.
Filling different spaces
full of light and shadow.

Jan Porter

The Betrayed Lover

An image lurks beside me,
A dark, frightening shape.
Leaning, taunting, pulling me closer,
I cannot escape.

I'm miserable, depressed, lonely,
Hurt, betrayed and I feel alone.
I'm frightened of my own feelings,
They're feelings that I can't condone.

I want to kill, to stop these thoughts,
They said his rejection was the workings of fate,
But still I know that I am living,
In the terrifying shadow of jealousy, anger and hate.

Rochelle D Rabin

Centering

If I reach out,
will you grab me?
Steady me?
Balance me?

Or if I reach out,
will you push me?
Topple me?
Uproot me?

If I leave,
will you laugh?
Enjoy the space?
Ask me back?

Or if I stay,
will you laugh?
Create more space?
Close me out?

I think I think too much of you.
Of what you may
or may not do?
Time to switch off.
Regroup, retreat,
and finally,
be graceful in defeat.

Alyson Faye

Barrabas Parting

No tears, love. What time is it?

I married once before.
Did you know that? A mute girl,
with hands like the wings of doves.

I gave up treachery for her.
said nothing against Rome for years
and now it seems I have
nothing left to say.

- Is this water? It tastes
foul as horsemilk. I wish
you'd cook lark's livers again
and bring me wine, to sweeten
my stinking breath. But larks
are rarer now, and wine full of death.

I climbed the hill of Golgotha
once. The sky rose cloud from cloud.
The sunlight was a crucifix
across my shoulders, and the dust
ran with our sweat. They called me
thief, thief and traitor.

On the hill of Golgotha
there was a man
with eyes like cities
and he died. I was condemned
and lived. Why was that? I think
it was a miracle.

Now, now. Where's my sight?
Quickly, love. Look for me.

How the shadows play
in the volumes of the light.

Fletcher Cooper

The Quantocks - A Lovers' Quarrel

After the rain a hushed expectancy,
Like lips half-parted, hangs on coomb and hill.
Along the red loam pathways, puddle-starred,
In pools of rust the tumbled clouds stand still
And pines with heavy fragrance load the air.
So my whole being pauses, waits for thee.
Mute are those strings that anger yesternight
To noisy discord plucked, and mute shall be
'Til quivering at thy familiar touch
They tremble in love's melody again.

Hark how the throstle and the linnet fill
With dancing notes this silence after rain.
The hour and place are big with signs. I cry,
And nature echoes, calling to the tryst.
Our quarrel, like this stormwrack, shall give place:
Thy raindrop tears to sunshine shall be kissed.

Norman Hurst

Freedom?

They're living together the Jones' and Smiths'
In north and south, in east and west
An open arrangement, so I'm told,
No ties that bind, no vows to irk
And baby mistakes or wistful whims
The state must surely care for them
For freedom is all and all they seek.

They're living together the Jones' and Smiths'
In north and south, in east and west
Living for free on benefit
Free to make love to whom they wish
Free of constraint of loyalties claims
Free to take all and never give.

They're breaking up the Jones' and Smiths'
In north and south, in east and west
Such brief encounters, so I'm told,
Free to be lonely once again.
Free to find yet another mate
Free to start living this dreary round
Of living together the Jones' and Smiths'

Dennis H Jackson

A Smooth Departure

I ironed his shirts
Then I left him.
Undemanding work
Frees the mind's eye.

So much room for thought
In creased cotton.
Made it easy to
Tell him drip-dry.

Polly Heyes

Lament

Here now am I - a halfmad minstrel
mewed in a phantom court
watching the dry words swirl
in the whirled dust
at the wit's end of a dream.

Mourning am I the livelong love-long
dream of an aching youth
dead in the ghost-hung hall
of a long grief
and a blind indifference.

Empty am I - the half-lived lovesong
hangs on a broken lyre
now when the moon Queen calls
a ritual feast
I'm but a serving man.

Only a serving man.

Lee Sheldrake

Rebirth

Warmth that was buried deep within was suddenly reawakened
not as if by magic - but by the sincerity of others!
Recent events dulled any confidence one ever had
made one question ones beliefs to the full
But no one person has the right to make one experience this
climbing this mountain uses all the strength within
And one finds this hidden power of survival, reaching the top
seeing new horizons and reaching out!

Having oneself think something was wrong within
turmoil against turmoil - slowly destroying any self confidence
one had, until the bottomless pit has been reached
Steadily sinking but friends refusing to let you sink
pull you up gradually, at a pace one never falls back on to !

All are human - but trust is earned, not a given right
having this broken can be like an image cracking
the full length of life's mirror - never to be mended!
But, my friend, you do overcome these scars that at a time
seem to be with you a lifetime
Most of all you succeed in another of life's chapters
and it is the actions of others that destroy
your feelings of old forever - and are reborn!

B J Allen

Polite Promises

It should have been climactic
Me under hot towels say;
You punctuating our association
in bullets from a passing car.

Or music rising over wet tarmac;
out of touch fingers slowly
folding from your tail lights.

That, perhaps, would have been
something to tell our future.

Instead I recall polite promises
and that late, last bus
out of your life.

Tony Noon

Duet of Thoughts

Her story
There he lies beside me
my one time Sir Galahad.
Heaving like a beached whale
and snoring again.
He means nothing to me now
and holds no attraction for me,
this man I once loved
and promised to stay faithful to.
He is obese and uncaring
and I hate him for sharing,
the rest of my life.

His story
She hates me now
I can feel it every day.
Just because I'm older and fatter.
She is always on a diet
trying to stay thin
taking care of her skin,
and worrying about her looks.
She still looks good to me,
I love her.
And want her always
to be part of my life.

Kathy Cox

Breaking up

Two lonely people, defeated, despairing
helplessly locked in intercourse born of habit;
two desperate people, floundering, confused,
raging, denouncing, guiltless, protesting;
two very nice people, bewildered, rejected
unwittingly programmed to self destruct
a fateful alliance of duplicate needs
traumatised partners struggling to understand
swollen with melancholic self pity
trapped between walls of tangible stress;
knee deep in the tattered shreds of passion
a consummate affaire past its 'Best Before' date
sickness invading hearts and minds
a contagion of deceit and mistrust
half truths and untruths, accused and accusing;
love drowning in bitterness, weighed down by hate
vituperative defiance, clandestine revenge;
two lovers torn asunder, agonising
snared by the past, afraid of the future
unwilling to face the final solution -
breaking up.

Jan Free-Gore

Friend, you Must be Sad

In the tears that swell a rancid
stream, in the daggers from your
passive eyes, in the crisies that have
made you mild:- you will see that you
are not forsaken, you will find the
strength to paralyse your fear.

In the whisper that suppresses wails, in
the lies that salt a fated wound, in the
losses that you cleanse away: there will be
the shade of petered sun, there will be
an everlasting eve.

In the touching which is frozen in, in the
teeth you rake from passion's fire, in the
questions you have asked to death: there
is an end to infinite pain, there are
shallows set beyond a deep despair.

Vincent M De Souza

The Tablecloth Trick

At the show
the conjuror stands
behind a table silver set.
The snare drums roll,
he tugs the cloth,
and nothing moves at all.

Next week
we imitate the trick,
but make mistakes.
You pull the cloth from under me,
and something breaks.

Nick Daws

Lover Mine, This is Our Love

See how the clockwork of the unfurling fern
strives to escape the earth's warm embrace

see how the shapes of swallows
become darting fish in vast sunlit oceans
seeking, seeking

see how the berry burns to fall
see how the skylark yearns to break her heart

see how the porcelain cloister of the flower
trembles for death

see how the emerald laminated beetle
hurries to death

see how the gossamer of the mayfly
is breathless for the sun to set

see how the globe turns lovingly to night

see how the bright star burns itself into night

see how our fingers interlock into a cage
and can never be too close

lover mine, this is our love.

Tobias Hill

Khayyam

Slipping from our rosy daybreak bed
I sidle down the corridors of dawn,
turning my burning head
uncertainly, believing you're still mine.

Your tousled hair, one cheek a creamy red,
sweet mouth yet forming an exploratory yawn.
Beside me, singing in the wilderness -
my erstwhile daily bread and weekly wine.

I catch my breath, and grasp a steady bough -
O Paradise, were tenderness enow . . .

Mal Jordan

A Silent Scream

The parting is amicable
I tell friends
with a smile.
So why this silent scream
of anger.
As deep as a cancer.
Yet threatening to erupt
with the megaton force
of a nuclear bomb.

Maureen Reynolds

Going Without

long time memories of lonely nights
come back to shadow me
pen to paper
music in my ears
I stream out testimonies of love
and belonging
to fill my hollowness
silk and velvet words with multicolour pens
on multicolour papers
purple petunia cards
and tapes
are all I have
in between deeper longings to be held
touched in your way especially

inadvertent tenderness from strangers
(fast becoming friends)
act as tiny dambusters
the torrent of which I would spend on you
my own hands stroke my own curves
and darker shades of skin
missing you is a tightness in my throat
an earache, a hunger of my senses
as I dream of riding home again
to your wet-me-up smiles and styles.

Dorothea Smartt

Assignation

Flykiller
hung about the room
Stuck to the unclean sheets.
The rusty fan was groaning
Clockwork rotations meted out the time
So much and then no more.
I felt your huddled shape
Knew ev'ry hillock all the curves
We both suspended time.

No single soul has been in here
Not for a year at least it seemed
The faded photos freckled with the damp
The armchair rocked on damaged legs.
The dust a blanket on the shelf
The carpet's weft and warp destroyed
By countless feet who used this room before.
Too rare a thing for us.

You took your plane down south
Towards the coast, left me alone
To hug the afterglow that fades too soon
And turns to salt
A column of unspent desire.

Ilse Danby

Bereft

I'm peeling potatoes. Soil grits my hands.
Dirty water swills in a blue, plastic bowl.
The last fat vegetable rests on my palm
as he clears his throat,
'Sue'
Why does he sound so strange?
'Sue. There's no easy way to say this.'
Say what? Why is he diffident today?
The potato stares up at me.
My frozen fingers clasp the knife.
'Sue, please turn round.' I peel on,
jab the sharp point into the eyes,
squeeze the hard flesh until white knuckles shine.
'I'm sorry.'
Don't say it!
'I'm sorry. I'm going. I've met someone else.'

I lie crying, mind a spinning top
whipped by his betrayal.
I'm peeling potatoes . . .

Hilary Tinsley

The Marriage Game

Windows shatter from blows of rage.
Children cower, flushed with shame.
It's just the turning of a page
in the marriage game.

Did she do it just to taunt him?
Did he leave her for too long?
Did she do it just to bait him?
Her morals never were too strong?

Why unfaithful? Could she gauge
his reaction. Oh what shame.
It's just the turning of a page
in the marriage game.

Did she do it just to hurt him?
Did she care that it was wrong?
Did she do it just to tame him.
Her morals never were too strong.

Windows shatter and at this stage,
Neighbours ask, 'Who is to blame'?
It's just the turning of a page,
In the marriage game.

Lilian Parker

Ending it all

When you said you were leaving
I felt like ending it all.
The idea of jumping off a bridge
Seemed like a good solution
Until
Someone tied a rope to my feet
Said:
'Bungy jumping isn't free mate!'
And then
Charged me ten quid.
Our relationship is worth more than that.
I love you
Let's give it another chance.

Philip Segar

Her Wreath

Blue matches his eyes
Yellow isn't him
Red mirrors his temperament
Grey is really grim
Black to suit his hair
Orange shocking tie
Lilac colour flowers
For the girl who stole my guy.

Shelagh Shannon

Full Time for us

It's full time for us dear,
the final whistle has blown.
There are no more away games,
no more fixtures at home.

Our love match has ended.
You showed me the red card.
I did one foul too many.
You came down on me hard.

Caught me in another league
with my muddy shorts down,
playing with the opposition
on another pitch in town.

It was only a friendly.
I didn't mean any harm.
just discussing new tactics,
just studying the form.

Only trying out new tackles
and bending the off-side rule,
showing my full-back position
and how to put one in the goal.

It's the sidelines for me now.
The small boy behind your net.
But - any chance of a replay?
Can't you forgive and forget?

'You're out of the team darling,'
she shouted down the 'phone.
'The season is truly over.
The final whistle has blown.'

David Wilkins

Break Point

Her house, her life, all orderly;
ruled precisely by the neat arrangement
of time and furniture.
Putting out for summer, drawing in for winter,
dusting, doing, thinking: a contrapuntal comfort.

He was neither organised nor clean.
He could talk to cows, be moonstruck, use a scythe,
hear the brittle music of the stalks
falling in their pattern. He could squelch in winter mud,
let spring arrive in its own time,
procreate, and eat untidy meals.

Yet she had said 'I do.'
He had vowed to cherish her till death
- that traitor - did them part.
They would not wait so long:
nothing is more vulnerable than vows.

Audrey Harbord

Regression

Sub-consciously I disconnect the reasoning
between my behaviour and my past.
Expectations of a pain, hurt and destruction conquer
the need of love.
Without contemplating destroying a chance of sharing
my self dependency I run away
from the sun.
Scared of catching cancer.
My strength is enhanced by success
and the vulnerability of others.
I see my weakness and manipulate coldly.
Inwardly laughing.
Questioning who is really losing.
Wondering who is in control.
My balance reaching perfection.
My equilibrium refusing to be swayed by
normal emotions which weaken your train of thought.
Constantly running.
Retreating from truth and ugliness of being valued.
Depending on the unreliable danger for security.
Questioning who has won.
Facing the alternative, no painless pairing.
Tears from in her thoughtful eyes and gives her the strength.
Her past encourages her to keep running.
Ripped and destroyed.
She locks the door.
No-one can enter.
It's over again, the barrier is rebuilt.

Carol Reynolds

Locked Within the Attic

The curtain of cobwebs cannot
Obscure past memories, which lie
Neatly stacked in cupboard and drawer.

Within the satin folds of my
Wedding dress lies etched a sense of loss,
And the shadow of Miss Havisham
Falls over this corner of the room.

I rock the cradle to rock away
The sorrow; to ruffle the air
Which holds your presence in camera.
Child of love, child of death,
Child of memory.

The disturbed past flies like dust to
All corners of my mind to teach
Me again that today is tomorrow
And tomorrow is yesterday.
The curtain of what might have been
Obscures all future dreams.

Sue Gerrard

Middle and Both Ends

It was . . .

Butterflies and colours,
Waterfalls and morning mist,
Dew-dripped cobwebs,
Clouds and roundabouts.

Then suddenly . . .

The empty shell of a laughing clown,
A door without its slam,
Lidless pots and potless lids
Rounds-without-abouts.

So I . . .

Sewing thread, knitting needles,
Bricks and stepping stones,
Red horizons, rainbow ends,
Roundabouts and bends.

That's about the middle and both ends of it!

Jennifer Greenway

Lost

The road was blocked
with worry and strife,
Clouds hid love from view,
Rocks stood tall and mountains high,
Too steep to climb alone.
I stumbled and fell
on that lonely road,
Lost, with no will to go on,
But a stranger stopped
to give his hand
and guide my steps a while.
The road ahead was full of twists,
The rocks cut deep with pain,
But this was the road
I had chosen to walk
So on I went, alone

The road ahead split two ways
My footsteps faltered with hope,
That the one I'd choose
Would lead me home
Where happiness shed its warmth.
The sun shone bright
Each step I took,
The road straightened before me,
Trials are past and there is love
With arms embracing me dearly.
I'm no longer lost, nor afraid
to travel along life's road,
With love walking beside me
No more will I wander alone.

Shirley Silman

Solitude

Sitting in a lonely room
playing my stereo
half listening to music
mind far away
In, the what used to be
wife, children and home
lost in my mind
gone in reality
divorced from the world
outcast by society
nothing but me alone
with 'Brothers in Arms'
coming from the speakers
on the stereo
no one to share my remorse
a bottle of cheap wine
slowly deepens my depression
I try to read Jack Higgins'
'Cold Harbour'
with an equally cold heart.

Myk Jonson

Crisis

Has there ever come a time in your life
When you don't know where to go,
When you're lost
And don't know what to think,
When your mind is going slow,
Where giving up seems the easiest way,
Keep on walking that long lonely road,
Will you find gold at the end of your rainbow,
Or are you destined never to know.

Divina McGonigal

When Death Comes Calling

A screech of wheels, a swerving, no time to wonder
the terrifying sound of steel tearing, breaking asunder.
Then came that wondrous sailing soaring slight
But as in my dreams down I came, crashing, falling
the hard merciless ground sending screams roaring.

Knock . . . knock . . . knock . . . knock (softly)

Dark fleeting images beckoning with all white faces
calling me softly, white walls, unrealistic places.
A murmur of strangers voices, not the one I needed
in my shadowed out of time land of pain I pleaded.
Please come my love, please come . . .

Knock . . . knock (slightly louder)

At last a remembered touch, but harsh words calling.
Don't go! Don't go! What will happen to me.
How can I manage on my own. Tell me. Tell.
Ranting and raging with a blaming selfish plead.
Yet sweet words of love were my only need.

Knock . . . knock (firmly)

Hold me. Tell me you will always love me. Only me.
Sweet words of love, of praise. Is that too much,
I ask of the dark stranger with the cold, cold touch.
A black beckoning shadow knowingly tearing me apart.
Does anyone care about the breaking of my heart.

Knock . . . knock . . . knock (loudly)

Now comes the final choice, will I go or should I stay
Will the breaker of my heart really miss me if I go away.
Alone in bitter darkest solace still I cry and weep.
My battle lost, I drift into empty, empty sleep.

M Finney

Seven Days of Love

On Sunday he loved me
On Monday he was unsure,
Tuesday was the beginning of
Restlessness by day four,
On Friday he was happier
On Saturday he was great
He said he was sorry,
I told him it was too late.

Keely A Nethercott

Unsuccessful Attempt

Driving to Snowdonia
our rescue team
slipped like scree
into separate valleys.

Gripping hands
across the arete
our fingers held,
between gear changes.

We zipped together clever
eight tog sleeping bags
and clattered into the night.
Two slates chipping keen edges
against sharp memories.

Your morning opened
at a pain grey face
I could not brighten.
Love seized.

Under the bonnet
my tears hiss goodbye
on an over heated engine.

Kevin Brewer

Like Distance

The tortured voices of rain and window,
Like cold hands that tremble
Touch, but pass no intimate remark,
And stay the silver tongues of discourse.

Then, silver against the moonlight,
A host of fears become knives
That terrorise my sleep,
And cut chill the warmth of slumber.

Warm hands suffer cherished faces
To sting, like the caress of a betraying kiss,
Breaking familiar horizons
Upon a cascading rhetoric, like distance;

Until my words, like distant mirrors
Reflecting jumbled images, realise at last
Their abuse of language,
Allowing the night its tortured silence.

Philip J Faulkner

Alone Again

A void exists where my heart once dwelled.

Misled by vivid imagination,
Which constantly strives to satisfy my desire to be loved,
I felt that I could love you:-
I thought we were in love . . .

Love herself was personified in you -
You possessed her soul and spirit
Spreading joy wherever you went.
But disillusion now rushes to greet me,
forcing me to face reality:-
You never really loved me.

Despondency hugs me,
Disappointment shakes my hand,
And once again loneliness, pain and heartache arrive;
They are now the only 'friends' I have.

It seems that I was merely the victim of a burning infatuation,
And as the last flame flickers and fades,
The dying ashes tell another story
Of my solitary existence,
Where I feel so unwanted, so unloved . . .

Jenny Prescott

Public Parting

The family had already read it,
he could tell, the way they looked.
'We can still go on the honeymoon
since it is already booked.'
She'd agreed to getting married
now she wanted to be free;
did she have to use a postcard
open there for all to see?

A proper letter with some effort,
a studied thought on page congealed,
folded firmly, stamped and posted
contents decently concealed.
That would have shown some dignity,
clothed his hurt in dark attire;
let him know she was aware
of how she'd thwarted his desire.

She'd entranced him from the start,
used her charms as a spur
to urge on a passion in his heart,
that made him want to posses her.
Now she'd used a ball-point pen
to tell him not to be upset,
'I just don't want to be married,
at least not to you - and not just yet.'

Rosemary Rogan

Confessions

Pour me another one Landlord, a stiff one and not watered down,
My story is not worth remembering, so here in your spirits I'll drown.
No plans have I to leave this bar room, there is just no place to go,
And I'm weary of walking the City, with my feeling and ego so low.

Pour me another one Landlord, and make it a double one please,
She's left me you know for another, my life is over I'm free . . .
Free of her flirting attentions, her attractions to all other men,
Her lashes, her smiles and her beauty, her figure, her eyes, her soft skin.

I should be happy she's left me, I should be glad to be free,
But life stretches bleak to the future; ah, that's what's the matter with me.
I would have given her everything, if everything would have made her stay,
All I asked was that she should be faithful, is that so much to repay?

I guess even I didn't know her, though I did try hard to recognise
Her thoughts, her dreams and her feelings, but it was really in her eyes . . .
They held a secret longing, that had nothing to do with me,
And the more I came to love her, the plainer it was to see . . .
That one day she would leave me, she who felt oppressed and bored,
Not for her our simple life together; a life which I had adored.
So pour me another one, Landlord, there's just nothing more to say,
I am sick, I'm twisted and bitter, since the love of my life went away.

You may say I am better without her, and the torment one day will subside,
But that won't stop me loving her, and so from myself I will hide.
Hah, pour me another one, Landlord, I've confessed enough for this night,
Let the bourbon come to my rescue so my sadness can briefly take flight . . .

But before I down this whisky, let me tell you once more so you'll know,
That life will never be the same without her
Now let the alcohol flow.

Annette McFarline

I Talk to Myself

Loneliness once again my ready companion.
Look at that face in the glass, pitiful.
I give a toast to us, the sad millions.
What have I done, what have I done wrong?
I treated her like a lady, I worshipped her.
Just to hold her again, to be seen in her eyes again.
I long to, I long to.

Look at this room - plastic,
No atmosphere, everything's bloody plastic.
Almost two quid a pint, two quid, the robbers.
I'm almost skint, what do I get for my money?
Songs of yesteryear, Cher and that gormless Sonny,
I've got you babe, huh! You've got to laugh.

Look at my life, misery, sheer unadulterated misery.
Nothing goes right, never has done, never will.
Oh Sarah you torture me, you eat away at me.
I feel you inside my head.
I can't sleep, I can't eat.
I feel so sad, so sad.
I talk to myself, am I going mad?

All I ever wanted to do was to love you.
And for you to love me.
To love and to be loved, that's all.

Francis Paul Farnworth

ice breaking

with my head
full of strategy
and my heart
full of romance
I took a chance
on the telephone
breaking the ice

but then I found
your line engaged
more than twice

Malcolm Rayment

Overflow

Your kiss has not yet left my brain
but hibernates
in the deep waters of my despair.
Your river flows
unchartered, unhindered
along the channels of my mind,
as I wade through pools of neglect.

You left on a wind's sigh,
your breath suspended in wispy circles
through my quiet valleys.

Now, the dark veil of memory
engulfs, floods out
that tiny stream of hope.

I flow gently, slowly,
through the upper reaches
of my soul, away
from your raging torrents.

Lorna Grinter

The Bitch

She ran off
with another
her lover
the bitch,
she made me feel dirty and cheap.
I swore that I'd kill him, if ever I saw him
the slimy
two faced
little creep.
Then we met four months later,
at a party,
'Where's your lover?' I snarled in her face,
'In the toilet,' she replied slightly shaking,
a worried look coming over her face.
Outside the toilet I waited with anger, building up till I thought I'd explode
when the flush went I took off my jacket, all my venom about to unload.
The door seemed to move in slow motion. My teeth I had clenched very tight
my arms hanging loose by my side, clenched fists turned my knuckles quite white
When the door had finally opened, some said that I turned deathly pale
for the bloke that I'd wanted to murder,
turned out to be a *female*.
My wife she stepped in, in between us,
'I'm sorry, I should have told you,' she sobbed
'This is mitch, the one I've been seeing.'
It felt as though I'd been robbed
Not only had my wife gone and left me,
but my revenge had been taken as well,
for I was taught you should never hit women,
but as I swung, I thought
what the hell . . .

J W Nevill

The Promise

You promised me that you would never hurt me,
That you loved me,
I would be safe to trust myself to your care,
Which I did, but what of love? Love was seldom there.
You hurt me in so many different, painful ways,
From your cold, uncaring attitude,
Your violent anger at people and the world,
To your moody and explosive days.

I was patient, understanding of the turmoil afflicting your mind,
I tried always to bring light and love to you,
But you could never find peace with yourself, or anything else,
I tried always to be kind,
No one could have loved you more than I,
But the love I trusted and gave to you quite freely,
You set out to destroy, I know not why.

You dealt out so much emotional shit to me,
Realisation dawned at a later date,
There was no real love in your twisted mind for me, only hate.
You were incapable of feeling real love for me,
Only able to hate and envy my inner peace and tranquillity,
What a sore thorn I must have been, continually in your side,
But my love you finally destroyed,
With the abuse of drugs, deceit and lies,
My inner peace sustains me well,
Whilst you in your darkness, will continue to dwell.

Shirley Boyson

Have a Guess

'I spy with my little eye something beginning with C.'
'C,' you say.
'Yes,' I say.
You give up without even a guess
And tell me to stop messing about.
'Let me give you a clue -
It's to do with you and me.'
'C,' you say.
'Yes,' I say. 'Let me hear you say something beginning with C'
'Candle,' you say.
'No,' I say.
'Are you sure?' you say with a smirk.
'Yes, I'm sure, we don't have candles any more,
Shall I tell you?
No, I'll give you one more clue -
It's what you're showing now.'
'How?' you say.
'By the way you're drawing further and further away from me,
And yes it begins with C,
It's to do with losing,
That's the last clue I'll give to you,
Got it?
Why haven't you?
It's easy, something beginning with C,
Go on try a guess.
No?
Well it's carelessness.'

Ian J Blackman

Resuscitation

The fill-dyke fields are empty.
Turned,
clodded and cold.
Waiting.
I, am halt,
in this stayed lark-mist.
Stopped.
Arrested.
It has been so,
season on season.
No resuscitation.
No jolt to life.
Now, here,
for a breath
drowning spring cries out,
reaching from the ocean
of forgetfulness
and I long to rescue us,
Spring and I.
But,
If this stealth morn
should start my pulse,
then with the throb
is pain revived,
such as the cut
which severed
golden celandine
to press
within a page's
memory.

B C Godfrey

Untitled

Uncomplacently I sat upon the sand,
Smelling the salt air and wiggling my toes.
I cried and shouted,
Whopped and yelled your name -
Defiantly at the sea.
And a seagull cried back,
It appeared lonely and lost,
Like me.

Kevin James Moloney

Disbelief

Wrapped in conjugal sheets,
shadows of the evening cast the nape of your neck
across the pillow.
I stretch out to touch your soft skin
but my hand melts into cold empty shadows.

Gently I cry your name,
only the wind answers with whispers of disbelief.

A silent tear falls upon the pillow,
and for an instant the scent of your sweet perfume
fills my head, and once again you're here
shrouded in my gentle reign.

Ian Shaw

On Adam's Retirement

Now Eve can manage on her own,
Adam's not needed any more.
She's better off now she's alone,
the crèche provided by the law.

No need for love with IVF
no need for special day in white.
No need to feel that carnal breath,
no need for the romantic night.

Now Eve's an independent girl,
Adam's part's no longer required.
No need for the sexist skirt twirl,
the golden ring is undesired.

'Let's put all the men in their place,
consign them all to one mass grave.
Then proudly walk with female grace,
imagine all the work we'll save!'

No need for love this modern day,
no marriage leads to no divorce.
I grieve silently with unseen dismay
as I watch progress take its awful course.

Simeon Jebb

Loki

Give me another space in time
and I will atone these misadventures.

Take me to the forge and place
burning coals on these plagiarist eyes.

The cry of 'Sorry', echoes down the telephone,
ripping, into your ear-drum.

The wrenched guttural motions
are ploughed electric-reality.

And Valhalla is falling
under Thor's hammer.

Creases weld in asphyxiation.
Blunt memory origami.

And the heartbeat paces
with a golden jaguar.

For what is sold from under us
is rancid forgiveness.

That will not forget.

Nicole Brannan

A String of Pearls

Round her neck a string of pearls
So wantonly she wears them,
Each one denotes a lovers tears
Now haughtily disdains them.
I gave to her that string of pearls
And round her neck I placed them,
And swore that through the coming years
Our love would surely bless them.
But what is life but hopes and fears
And love that could deceive them,
A cultured love no heart can keep
The truth will aye displace them,
But true love runs forever deep
And endless does embrace them.

A J McDonald

Water Into Wine

I am a vessel,
Made to hold water
An earthen vessel of little value,
Except to the thirsty.

I used to hold water,
Cold, plain, tasteless water.
She was the water.

She was drawn from the well
And poured into me.
I held her and we waited.

At the wedding feast he came.
He came and turned my water into wine.
Sweet, smooth, full of body, the best wine of all.

I changed. Still an earthen vessel,
But now I had precious wine.
How proud I was.

I would not be poured out.
'I am the vessel, the wine is mine!'
I would not be poured.

He came again in sadness.
With great sorrow he smashed the vessel
And the wine flowed free.

It nourished the earth
And washed his feet
As he gazed upon the broken vessel.

The wine flowed over every piece,
Washing the shattered vessel with love
And passed out into the world.

Graham Hitch

A Gardener

A broken up gardener I am, what shall I do?
A fickle love I have, but I will not forget
She had a lovely smile, but she was not so true,
Although so refreshing, like water from a jet.

She is my Geranium, my beautiful rose
My daffodil, love-in-the mist, and hollyhock,
She's my water lily and my lovely primrose,
Also peony, orchid and sweet smelling stock.

We were like two plum trees, we grew up together
Close to each other like double begonia.
They now plant her in a pot with coloured heather
And I'm left to die just like the magnolia.

I'm like a sweet pea, helplessly lost in its cane,
Or like a cucumber or tomato in pots
A broken up gardener, now working in vain,
Withery and dying, absolutely, just rots.

G M Albon

Broken Promises

You've gone, and sadly I had to go through your things.
Letters tied with ribbon
A small gold ring.

I read the last one first, reluctant to intrude.
It was written in pencil, the paper very crude.

My dear you're twenty one now
It's time to settle down.
I feel that I must tell you
That I won't be around.
I like to take a drink,
As all us sailors do.
I'd have to give it up I know,
If I were to marry you.
Fondest regards to your mother
I'm sure she'll understand.

I can't explain the anger, I felt for you inside.
The independent woman I'd looked upon with pride.
Perhaps if I'd looked closer
I might have seen your pain.

Perhaps you even blamed yourself,
Were you very insecure?
Was that why you spent your time alone
For sixty years or more.

Emma Shaw

A Letter from an Old Friend

A letter from an old friend
he left unopened
because he knew
the news would be bad.

Leaving it at home
he went out to drink
knowing of no other place
to sit and think.

Drinking all evening
he remembered times good
and nothing there was
to empty his heart.

Back home to the room -
hell room with the news -
the closed letter: a picture
framing his life.

He lay on your bed
unable to sleep,
invoked shadows to draw
dark veils over life.

A letter from an old friend
he left unopened
knowing full well
why from me it came.

A letter from an old friend . . .

Yes, he had known
about you -
and he had known about me.

Geoffrey Winch

The Eating of Britain

His body was full of bullion.
Gold grew on his teeth,
He swallowed flocks of seagulls.
Surrounded by bagpipes,
He ate the Grampians.

Like a piggy bank with wings,
He flew with ease.
The cries of Britons,
He chose not to hear.
He believed in privacy,
The stilling of blood.
The beautiful legs of women,
He sweated in the long afternoons.

His breath swept over the Brecon Beacons.
In newspapers his name never appeared.
His spokesmen stopped mobs from forming.
He saw himself simply as an owner,
As the single banker,
He broke forever,
The corrupt dictum;
That Britons never shall be slaves.

Brent Hodgson

The Braer

The storm caught her unawares, the Braer,
Lurching her ungainly way through heavy seas,
Tossing her crude cargo uneasily
As she ploughed her way amid swirling breakers
That raced to hurl their might
Upon the rocky Shetland shore.

Desperately, she fought the tide,
Bucking and pitching helplessly in the teeth of the gale,
Crashing drunkenly among short steep waves,
And reeling at the power of the towering rollers
Which carried her along
Upon their steep, undulating swell.

Uselessly she searched for help
Across the wilderness of empty sea,
But the wind howled,
And the savage crests crashed across her bows,
Bursting with spray,
Sluicing her decks,
And forcing her, screaming,
On to the predatory rocks
Which gouged her sides until she bled,
Pouring out her agony to poison the seas.

Silent sobs of shellfish throbbed through the deep currents,
Salmon leapt desperately within their prisons,
Seals, coated in the seeping, creeping horror,
Lay pathetically on the beaches
Waiting with helpless shags and seagulls
For man who poisoned them
To set them free.

Chris Jones

Storm

The first few drops fall from a cloudless sky.
Alarmed, she sees slow rings widen and fade
Across the lily pond, and with a cry
Enters the summer house, tries to evade
The grey clouds massing, wiping out the sun.
The sky weeps, streams grooving the dust-grimed pane;
A forked flash lights her dark, rain-barred prison.
Her cell affords no haven from the gale.

Her lover's letter crumpled on the floor,
She beats her fists against the unmoved pine
Her anguished cries drowned by the tempest's whine.
At last the tumult ebbs; through opened door
She steps, with tears on dewy-petalled cheeks,
Calm now, to face alone the loveless weeks.

Lucy Newsam

The Diamond Knife Tarnished

Bring, bring down, bring down the diamond knife
Which flashes through the heart-broken flames
Purging the Sirens' wail to the Lorelei
King; calling out his several screeching names
To the tragic, pregnant pause of a womb!
Antigone, frozen into Jocasta
Screams for the blood of Zeus to drip
Over her hair - the salt-soaked screen
Of grief - but Zeus has stepped into the shard
Splintered window of delusion as mortal love:
The mirror-self, leaving vanity to Oedipus' daughter!

Stroke, stroke across, stroke across the diamond;
The diamond vision to whom crystal vowed the glory:
The glory that is gripped in bright-faceted hands;
The glory of heart tragedy! Blind Homer in your dome
Sparkling haven write the Iliad for the dice of Caesar!
The visage floats into the bowl to drip
The zest of ecstasy in lovers' sighs:
Purdah over a plank of wood - the unclean
Miracle of Hyacinthus and Narcissus -

The diamond edge reflects rapture in the candle glow
Yet, startling twilight, swirled hands embrace sacrifice!
Rising from the quiet chaos of the slab;
Rising out of the wrecked effigy of Wotan;
Rising away from the mortal love to
Ascend into the brightness of her tear-stained navel.
The diamond nature of the knife, tarnished,
Drips slowly, succinctly their stolen life-breath . . .

Suzanne Stratful

Swansong

I feed the swans
Every dinner time
With my crusts.
Even though
I wasn't supposed
To be there.

I felt they brought me luck,
Even though
I'm not superstitious.
At least the swans
Didn't break my arm
With their beaks,
As they could've done.

The uneasy truce
The swans and I had made,
Was not unlike
Us.
But I was not convinced
That you were as easy to pacify,
That you would have blackmailed me
For far too much,
That's why I left.
Broken arms are easier to heal
Than broken hearts.

Lesley Marshall

Match Point

Wimbledon: wicked and alive again
Where tantrums personify flagrant men;
Where women gleam false-virginal in white;
Where lost Summer day meets the rain-filled night
And blips at the moment on this TV screen
Quite smothered in dust; that imperfect sheen
As grey as the mood that sets this flat room;
As wan as one might just dare to presume.

Then: loud cheers for a stinging-fast ace
Reverberate madly, swallow each place:
The superlatives whizz, faster than balls:
Commentary orgasm in Upper-Class drawls.
The camera pans, seeks appreciative grin:
Captures the face of ex-lover with 'him'.

Tom Miller

Fish on the Move

We watched the furniture get carried in,
A threadbare chair and a laundry bin,
The goldfish entered two by two,
You looked at me, I looked at you.

A month earlier, we'd been at the wedding,
And knew then where you were heading,
'Bale out now,' I longed to shout,
But the fridge went in, and the love went out.

Arguments put down to pressure,
Glossed over beyond all measure,
Teething troubles, it will pass,
A marriage through a looking glass.

You soon embarked on full scale wars,
Hurling insults and slamming doors,
Hurt and anger, tears and pride,
Helpless against a turning tide.

For eight months you acted out the part,
Greasepaint smile and heavy heart,
You threw in the towel with your final shout,
And we watched the furniture get carried out.

Julie Daly

Windswept

Passions flames dances with tears,
as volcanic love erupts with fear.
As storm clouds gather in life's blue skies
voices scream betrayed by lies.
Secrets waltz; witnesses one by one.
A fist waved in anger, brings on the rain,
a fools confusion and a downpour of pain,
We had times of drought and a flood or two,
but nothing as strong as this storm that brews.
A storm that will lift us then rip us apart
with a whirlwind so strong it will pierce through the heart.
We may try to take shelter in the love that we feel,
but the rafters are weak for our love is not real.
When lightening strikes we'll burn and we'll choke,
you know what they say there's no fire without smoke.
Well our fire is dead, our land barren and dried,
only our memories drowned in the tears that I've cried.
Like the wind you deceive with those stories you told.
Your warm sunny smile now turns me stone cold.
It's not that I mind what you've done with your life,
but I'd rather you did it with someone else as your wife.

Nicola Plumb

Lover's Lament

Would it have been any different,
If we'd ever really spoken?
I think not.
What we had in common was insecurity,
A need to hold on to one another.
This once outgrown,
Well, what now Lover?

West Princes Street Gardens

Unaware of trains waiting on Waverley
or crowds along Princes Street,
two lovers in a public park
where worlds have their beginning
orbit and every other function
in an embrace, a word or look.
Futures are for planning together,
and the beds in different towns.

Unaware in twenty years someone
browsing the all night bookshop
will hear among the half price pulp
a quiet background of forgotten songs,
arcing recollection of this same place,
recalling gardens, grass and love.

Unaware they will return, looking here,
triangulating castle, path and tree
to find where, one sweet spring of memory,
promises were made and passions begun.
Familiar views are rediscovered
yet searching cannot find the spot.
With weeds, grass seems coarser;
where, how did they lay so long?

If the lovers knew it would be so,
chiefly one would predict chagrin
someone makes their shrine a grave,
offence becoming moist eyed disbelief
at recognition it is one of them
and they have returned, alone.

Paul Berry

The Hour of Change

Lying in a rumpled sheet,
uncomfortable feelings cling to me.
You lie beside me asleep
I lie beside you hoping the clock will stop.
Past conversations irritate
good memories turn sour.
Fingers move around the face,
The hour of change is imminent.
I shut my eyes for the first time
Hoping when I wake I'll see your back still here,
Knowing if I touch it, you won't flinch.

Laurie Carmen

Bridled And Broken In

Chivalry is dead? Not at the beginning
though somewhere near the end.
Fairy tale, happy ever after - a must!
Like hanging clouds out to dry or taming the
storm, well, perhaps.
Perhaps for a while as rites take place kids
show face to bulge and play soul destroying games
Why? Because tradition dictates,
A period of complacency
No! there is no leniency
Another doormat eats the dust
what you thought was, isn't.
Plough onwards, ask no questions
a mental hide and seek ensue
alienation, confusion breed frustration
but where has chivalry gone to?
A mindless body, a pumping stone
once you were two now you're alone
with siblings siphoning your fun,
the vows and the ring were just a con,
struggling to stay sane among such betrayal and pain
with knowledge that you married Jeckyl and Hyde
with such revelation each seed of love died.

Clementine Withy

Burnt Out

Once the fire burned brightly.
The flames leapt and danced.
Gold, orange, red, yellow.
Its heat intense, melting,
Consuming all . . .

Now it's died down,
Dimmer, almost out.
Only the embers glow
Amongst a pile of ashes,
Fading . . .

Peter Burns

The End of Love

Love lies bleeding in the dust,
Within me just an empty void,
Only duty guides me now I trust.
It started with just being annoyed;
Anger built up, brick by brick,
Nourished by returned bitterness,
Until, under resentment, pride began to kick.
I felt valued less and less,
Within me love began to change,
To change its very shape and feel,
To acquire a different name,
And gradually, cease to be real.
Into my heart hatred crept,
It grew and grew like weeds,
Love at first only slept,
Then, silent to all pleads,
Love died, and, in its place,
Emptiness and woe,
With no remembrance of love's face,
I now look on my foe.

Jill Dyer

Parliament Square

My arm wound with his: a familiar clasp.
Walking as friends as we used to as lovers,
The lunchtime wine still warm in my mouth.
Our lips curving upwards from laughter, from flirting.
His affectionate kiss placed full on my lips.

Opens my eyes
Ribbons of longing flush through me
And are gone.

Recklessly, I lean forward to repeat
And receive instead a tactful repulse:
A squeeze of the shoulders, a kiss on the cheek.
For a moment I feel pain, and then I laugh
And we leave each other without looking back.

Angela Evans

The Torrent

Rain rain pouring down in torrents, running down hair ends
clinging to neck, damp clothes, make up running
nose bloated, eyes shut then open, flicking water
splashing, wading through, down pouring soaked, hair style ruined
birds nest come, all the time spent on washing rinsing blow dry hairspray
gone, in streams and musty clumps bedraggled drenched to the skin
oh for dryness warmth from within,
to be sitting by the fireside hot drink, dry, sheltered, shoes off
feet lying high, bibbing of car breaks silence . . .
a wave as it passes by, drenched to the ankles
will this rain please stop as I look at the sky.

Pat Jones

Stranded

Night spilled whispers of pleasure
For months through blackened lips,
Shadows lingered like spiders
Noiseless, elegant souls -
But now -
Breathe as hard as I can,
I need to know I'm still alive;
Stranded alone in this darkness
Cautious, isolated
So battered and bruised,
No precise, confident tricks.

Ingrid Blanchard

Picking up the Pieces

I used to think that you were my best friend
Other people told me that you were.
Now, I'm not so sure.
Best friends don't hurt each other the way you did me!
Or do they?

You left!

Throwing me aside like an old coat, you didn't need anymore.
Leaving me to suffer the agony of the pain you caused our marriage.
Leaving me to pick up the pieces of my life, that you broke.
Leaving me to explain to the kids, why, you punctured the ball of love
and security, held in the palms of their innocent hands!
But are they not the same kids, you swore you loved so much?
No-one, you said, would ever be allowed to hurt them, while you are
alive.

So?

What are you going to do about you?
What are you going to do about the hurt you've caused them?
Will you apologize to them for pulling out of their lives to live with
someone else?
I don't think so!
You've never apologized to me!
So, how can I expect you to say 'sorry' to them?
Well, it really doesn't matter anymore.
My pain is healing with time.
I'm stitching the pieces of my life back together again.
I've explained to the kids on my behalf, never yours!
They've accepted my words and love me the more for it.
They make me smile, when tears threaten my eyes.

I'm proud of them and I'm proud of me!
And look!
I've even made history.

I'm the 'Humpty Dumpty' that all the King's horses and all the King's men *did* put back together again!
I'm *Me*!

Patti Bancroft

The Little Old Lady of Bromley by Bow

Upstairs on the landing
A large house in London
Sits my little old lady of Bromley by Bow,
Looks down every morning
From half open windows
And sees all the pushing, impersonal people
Who pass by her windows, but none of them know
My little old lady
Looks down from her landing
In lost hours of living in Bromley by Bow.

Her hall has a picture,
The loves long forgotten
Of my little old lady of Bromley by Bow,
Her scrap book of sunshine
Of springtime and waltztime
Of children in braces and babies in rompers,
The bromide is fading but memories grow,
My little old lady
Throws sweets from the window
For children to gather in Bromley by Bow.

No doubt she is dreaming
Of someone to hold her
Is my little old lady of Bromley by Bow.
A sad smile she's wearing
A warm heart she's sharing
And sends all her suitors bouquets of her sunshine
So sailors may hornpipe and pipers may blow.
My little old lady
Calls out from her window
For someone to talk to in Bromley by Bow.

Chris Porteous

Bitter Harvest

Tender moments, now forgotten
Tempers frayed with time and stress
Forever stealing golden moments
One more kiss, a soft caress.

Once life was full of love and laughter
Sadly embers die and fade
No rich material for rekindling
Harshness loathing in loves place.

The call was strong, resistance weak
Returning you to family life
This heart struggles in stormy waters
Seeking refuge without strife.

'Never love an older man'
Maybe it was tempting fate
This 'other woman' loved him dearly
The words of wisdom came too late.

Flora M Cameron

This Time

Whenever we spoke of breaking up
It was really hypothetical
Since we knew about it only too well
And as language meant the
same to you and me
I really thought the chain
had snapped, we in our own circle,
A ring of arms,
Tight band of charms,
This time.

But as the weak links began to chink
memories spun back like catalysts
Stretching our credibility farther
Until the threads were
Beyond joining again.
Yet when the hurt recedes
eventually as it must, what
Is there but a
chance to repeat
This time.

It feels like casting off a disease
So familiar it's almost needed
To sustain a kind of biorhythm
A means of living
And when you are removed
Will my life improve or
Be lost within its emptiness.
Perhaps we should
have tried to make it
This time.

Sally Angell

Brittle

Our love, so brittle-boned,
has broken
as we knew it would;
the shattered pieces
crumbling peace
as battered lives
together cease
to flourish with
the fading of
our light . . .

Julia Lucie

Symbols

The sugar bowl you gave
White, the handle lemon shaped
Smashed, the sugar grains scrunch on the kitchen floor
I kneel to pick each minute bit
Too small to put together and to mend.
Tears, at the clumsy act
That stole another symbol of us two
Hand, that touches the green veined leaves
Trembles as my heart lets go
And breaks in many pieces like the simple clay.

Deirdre van Outersterp

The Letters

I can't forget the letters
Pulsating in my purse,
They're throbbing, fighting violently,
Struggling - even worse -
They're powerful and passionate,
Tender, kind and true,
All the things you ever said,
Your feelings old and new.

They're pleading with me, 'Mercy, please,
Don't do this dreadful thing.'
Ignoring this I find a place
Where birds are on the wing.
I shred the letters - throw them high -
'Confetti for the Birds'
And may they pick up little bits
Of 'Dearest' 'Darling' words.

But now I feel a deep regret,
My heart is full of pain -
I'm yearning for your letters, dear,
Please may we start again.

Josie Boot

Untitled

unprepared unthinking saying
something stupid off the cuff
blurting out my love
blushing embarrassed and hot
under the collar
and suffering for my honesty
not living in someone special's
pocket no one wanting to
live in mine - finding only
a snotty hanky there
to weep into
must learn to staunch
my tears and keep my
lip buttoned and not
wear my hasty heart
on my sleeve.

Jane Fell

Songlines

I remember you
In the warp and the weft
Of the black and white times,
The good and the bad.

Your wraith surrounds me,
Feather printing on my mind
With soft deft touches
The imprints of days and nights and twilights
Shared between us
In acts of love and lust and passion . . .
And gentle silences.

Yet I remember too
The wars we waged,
When clanging bells of bitterness and fury, even hate,
Erupted like hidden enemies springing into battle.

But with your passing
All the flint-edged shafts of desperation
Recede back into nothingness.

Then I remember
That once you loved me,
When your hand in mine
Signified some strange bond between us
Then . . . and now . . . and always.

And I miss you.

Mary Smith

Shattering Illusions

I looked into your brown eyes
And thought there were hidden depths
But I was wrong
There were only shallows.
I wanted to drown beautifully
In the oceans of your gaze
But I found when I tried
They were deep enough only to paddle
I dreamed of you constantly
But when I awoke
I found the dreams had more substance
Now I am sad
Because you can never match fantasy.
I am rich in my dreams
While you are poor in your reality.

Chris Davies

Birthday Card

An unsuspected surprise
Flopped through her letterbox
Reopening a rattlebag
Of mixed memories.

The Engagement party
Hugs below sultry moons
Candlelit Saturday nights.

Megashock when time bombs
Nearly brought down the stars.

Wine with womanising
Was a lethal cocktail
Too hot to swallow whole.

Despite apologies
Fruitbaskets and flowers
She would hold on to his`
Expensive diamond ring.

A phone call should scupper one
Last chance - the split was for real.

James Adams

Independence Day

Fewer than expected see the dawn of a new age,
Left behind their tortured aeons of pain,
Broke free from all conventions which kept them caged,
And vowed that things would never be the same again.

Things had gone too far; I couldn't carry on,
Could not endure the lie that I was living,
All hope of resolution had long since gone,
No reciprocation of all that I was giving.

New Year, new ideals, new start,
The time is nigh for me to break free,
I've realised that we're better off apart,
Your dominance just overshadowed me.

Our lives are heading off in different ways,
We'll leave behind this wreckage, this bloody mess,
There's nothing really left for me to say,
Except I hope, in time, you'll come to hate me less.

Vanessa Rivington

Got Away - Caught Again

As I sit, I think;
As I think, I weep.
As I weep, I rue;
As I rue, I seek.
As I seek, I wait;
As I wait, I wonder.
As I wonder, I hope;
As I hope, I try.
As I try, I fail;
As I fail, I find.
As I find, I hold;
As I hold, I grasp.
As I grasp, I love;
As I love, I care.
As I care, I rest;
As I rest, I sleep.
As I sleep, I dream;
As I dream, I wake.
As I wake, I lose;
As I lose, I know.
As I know, I cast;
As I cast, I hook;
As I hook, I cling.

Jock McGregor

Alone at Last

At last the peace and quiet I crave
so why does the house feel like a grave?
As I wander taking stock
no crumpled shirts or lonely socks.
The toothpaste plump, not twisted, lies
on splash free tiles which blind my eyes.
One pillow crumpled on the bed,
no dent where you have lain your head
On the drainer one mug and plate stand drying,
so why the Hell am I still crying?

Hazel Jones

A Barren Harvest

That small word 'if', induced a tiff
and tore their world asunder.
An argument, made them resent
each other . . . little wonder!

One chance remark, had set the spark
that kindled flame to fire.
With embers low, that once fierce glow
spelt death to sweet desire.

Statements uttered in the heat
often leads one to defeat.
Resentment in its fullest train
triggers action, quite insane.

Most break-ups seem to start like this.
Rose-coloured glasses, promised bliss.
But sadly neither Man or Miss
Will settle with a peaceful kiss.

Injured pride keeps them apart.
Estrangement leads to broken heart.
Yet common-sense could save the day.
Experience, would pave the way.

n Lee

Breaking Up

Sweet silence
after nightmare noise
and cold reproach.
This break
ends our
combustible
hell-havoc.

A separate silence
invades this space -
a soft wind
blows
and my dark glows,
grows
a sharp light.

Our orbital years
transcends my moon,
now black ash -
but one star
remains
to shine
as sweet revenge:

as parted -
the breaking up of
outworn habits,
casts away
love's flotsam -
as dust in space,
now sweet silence.

Gwynneth Curtis

I Lost my Love

I lost my love when Death had wreaked its pain,
Leaving me only the past to re-live again.

I met my love when both of us were foolish,
Strong in the innocence and beauty of our youth,
Flirtatious of eye, and fancy free of mien,
No serious thoughts of love, only sweet dalliance.

But when our eyes met in mutual appraisal,
A strange excitement coursed swiftly through our veins,
A feeling that somehow we had met before,
And a trembling at the touch of the other's hand.

Almost without our awareness there soon followed,
Walking on air days, proclaiming of vow days,
Rapturous joy of meetings, sharp pains of parting,
Followed by endless mutual messages of love.

Exchanged whisperings of sweet nothings,
Hand holding, lips meeting, arms entwined,
And two hearts beating in unison.

I loved my love, when the flush of youth had gone,
Surviving serenely, the ups and downs of life,
But I lost my love when Death had wreaked its pain,
Leaving me only the past to re-live again.

Winifred Roberts

Passing Time

In company,
dry-eyed -
all cried-out anyhow:
impassive mask
to veil the devastation underneath
by day.
At night
on sleepless, twisted sheets,
no passionate embrace,
no crying out;
just tears
uncomforted.

Clare Woods

The Signs The Hopes

Cigarette butts in the ashtray,
betraying my worry.
Raindrops on the windows,
counting my tears.
An empty glass on the sill,
showing my misery.
An ear waiting for the phone,
to express my love.

The butts pile up,
the rain keeps falling,
the glass is re-filled,
and the phone never rings.

Angela Gray

Subtle Hints of Demise

At the end of the line sits the surprise that
evokes no will to confront.
Don't fight the hidden shadows that follows
the lamplight in the night.
Beware of the subtle hinds of demise
Do not carry the burden alone
Find refuge in the lonely figure that spells help.
Do not be surprised if you recognise the face as yours.

Chinedu

Letter to Sam

Sam,
You are not dear to me any more.
In fact you've become a total bore.
I know you are having a steamy affair,
But I really don't care.

I hope she can stand your eternal snores and burps,
Your sweaty socks and grease stained shirts.
Fact is you have many irritating habits
Apart from expecting humans to be as sex mad as rabbits.

Don't promise the earth and give only a dime,
Don't hog the bathroom for an hour at a time.
Don't get home late and give no explanation
Then give her a slap if she dares to question.

Don't tell her you love her when you are seeing another,
And never say she reminds you of your mother.
Now that I have the complete picture of you,
Breaking up is so very easy to do.

Farewell Sam, I wish you well
I hope she has the courage to make your life hell!

Mary Gilby

Exposé

The last time I saw you
was at the end
of a wet, winter
Saturday afternoon
already
dripping dusk
when the market stalls
were disappearing.

You were surveying
the beauty
of the remaining
fruit stall
with that secret smile
on your face
so much in character
when you were feeling good.

We stood
side by side
in the rain
on light reflected pavements
in our rainproof
camouflage
exchanging polite
pleasantries.

I betrayed
my left over love for you
by talking too much
talking too much . . .

June Heather Cook

Bitter Tears

With bitter tears upon my cheek
I hurt so much, I cannot speak
Love we shared has faded so much
Leaving
Memories of your special touch
Which haunt me in my lonely hours
My tears cascade in painful showers
Of
Regrets upon my aching brow
The hurt is truly starting now.
So final
Were your words today
And wishing that you'll always stay
I cry my tears
I whisper words
To deafened ears
And sharpened swords.

Pollyanna

Void

Cohesive as pond life
Interactive, supportive,
We believed we were.

To watch and see if high tide's final wave
Would move the bluish shingle
Diversion enough.

Our unity and joy brought warmth
Even to the cold china egg
Ageless in the grey fowl's nest.

Freedom, fragmentation,
Now you are gone.
The single living touch I can endure
Is the tepid gentle mushroom
Of a stray cat's paw.

Jennifer McDonald

Missing You

found myself
talking to me
and although
every word I spoke
was true
I also found
I was missing you.

Malcolm Rayment

So Who's Deprived?

There was a time when they were glad
And grateful for the home we had
But now they have a lonely tea
And somehow fail to notice me.

At first they made a lot of noise
And left me playing with my toys
Yet now they hardly speak at all
And friends don't often care to call.

I'm sorry for the things they say
And hope they'll smile again one day
'Cause I enjoyed the times we had
When once I had a Mum and Dad.

Eric Burke

Help - My Body Break Up
Wanted - One Zip Fastener

Patiently I'm waiting for you to send for me,
Yet, I must confess, I am quaking at the knee.
If I only had a 'zipper' one could pull up and down -
As if I were a handbag one carries into town.
Yet, my somewhat different 'contents', or so it seems to me,
Are taken out, displayed and hung like toys on an Xmas Tree.
I wonder if they're fluorescent - or, even sprayed with glitter?
If they were tinsel trimmed would I be any fitter?

Oh! what a 'carry on', I'm a wizard at 'positions',
I only hope Dear Sir you are as good with your 'incisions'.
My modesty has vanished, I've been viewed both front and back.
By doctors old and young sometimes white and sometimes black.
Ah! well, I've got to face it so, chin up my dear,
You have a tip-top surgeon trust him and have no fear.
I still wish I had a 'zipper' - I don't want another scar,
But I'll come through smiling, surgeons being what they are.

Esther Hawkins

Loneliness

A void.
A lump that somehow can be solid and yet empty;
Nothingness; tangible, but tactile not.

And quiet,
Such silence as is audible
When all the little sounds are meaningless,
And bigger things are missed.

There is nobody to share with.
No soaking up of joys and disappointments;
A meal prepared, but minus that ingredient
Which is purpose.

Jennifer Churches

The Rhythm of You

Like a wet fire;
the music around me dies,
as my eyes,
meet the blankness of your glance.

'Blankness',
for coldness is far too harsh,
for anyone who's believed,
who's lived,
for Love.

The music still rich and strong,
my world empty of a song.

Zoe Dellous

End Game

Pawn to E4,
The game commences.
He throws the knife,
She sharpens her teeth.

Knights defence,
Repeated patterns,
He racks his mind,
She stifles a yawn.

En passant capture,
Ace in the hand.
Excuse me please,
I beg your pardon.

Topple the King,
End of the game.
Leave her alone
And summon the next.

Andy Gilbert

Act Too

Down the final curtain
A three part drama concluded
The excitable young girl
Exited, stage left;
A bit player
With delusions of stardom.
You return to me
Your former leading lady
Looking for the love
To repeat our romantic scene
But its jaded, faded
For I have moved on
Into another set
A totally new play:
My own top billing.

Marlene Morris

Old Lovers

Nervous glances
Where once we gazed
A creaking friendship
Where passion blazed.

A joke that once
Would make you smile
Now raises a puzzled
Enquiring brow.

Lips that knew
The other's kiss
Now drawn in lines
Of bitterness.

And stilted conversation
It seems
Replaces that
Which flew on wings.

P M Holloway

Adder on the Stairs

Red rings of kestrels
Falling:- sun-scarred
Dropping:- from heaven to hell.
Where are my gods?
What price silver?
Who served me poison?
On a cold night in June.
Capture by curtains
Madness in mirrors
Talking to teapots
Walking on walls . . .
Goodbye smart Judith
The days are too long
And the nights,
Too cold.

Barefoot in thistles
Stalling:- run-scared
Hopping:- from heaven to hell.
Where are my dogs?
What price cages?
Who stole my music?
On a cold night in June.
Savage by silence
Whispers in windows
Aching in ashtrays
Faking no falls . . .
Goodbye smart Judith
The days are too long
And the nights,
Too cold.

John Nelson Holmes

Me and My Guy

We're breaking up - me and my guy,
He's found another lover.
He loved me once - not any more,
It hurt me to discover.

Will she spoil him - just as I did,
Give in to his every whim?
Fool if she does - that's not the way
To keep and satisfy him.

He likes the chase - enjoys the race,
Climaxing in the capture;
Once he has caught - his lively prey
Cooler becomes his rapture.

She is welcome - to my old man;
I hope he gives her pleasure,
But knowing him - he'll drain her dry.
Of him I have the measure.

We're breaking up - me and my spouse,
A better soul-mate I've found.
I adore this one - he's such good fun,
And won't give me the run round.

He protects me - he respects me,
His one and only mistress,
And what is more - my Labrador,
Was born to faithfulness.

Irene Giles

Too Little

Words flung like acid in her face
Searing the skin and scarring the mind
Yet you ask
Did he beat you?
Her body curves in on her - a question mark
Her voice cannot shape
What about violence to the mind?

Once giggling eyes, now stupid with pain
She cannot parade her mind, torn of its moorings,
Like a bloody welt.
If she stays above water
You are not convinced,
If she drowns in her delirium
You rush in . . .

Too late.

Rahila Gupta

He Loves Me Not

You bastard! I hate you! How could you do this?
Ruined so much for one pathetic kiss.
Her blonde hair is lovely, but what about her spots?
Blue jeans so tight, I see you've got the hots.

I'm feeling great, got a new hairstyle,
but what is it I lack?
Do me a favour, when she throws you out,
don't come crawling back.

But I have to admit
I can't resist you,
I don't suppose she will.
So I quit.

Anne Butler

James

Now, if she thinks of him at all,
She thinks of him as James.
She'll find it hard now to recall,
That he had other names.

She called him luvvy pie and pet,
And precious angel love,
The sweetest person ever yet
Sent from the heavens above.

She called him gorgeous, honey mine,
Without whom I should die
And even something less divine,
The apple of her eye.

She called him ducks and dearie,
Each day from early dawn,
And he was never weary,
As she went on and on.

She called him jewel, lover man,
Her poppet, honeybunch,
She drooled as only sweethearts can.
Then came the awful crunch.

She left, it seemed just on a whim,
And quite without a thought
Of what might then become of him
Now that she loved him not.

No longer do his words enthral.
Extinguished are love's flames.
And, if she thinks of him at all,
She thinks of him as James.

Ken Walmsley

Today I Discarded Part of My Life

Today, I discarded part of my life.
I wrapped up the fear in an old paper bag
And placed it in the depths of my mind.
I buried the hate and the anger
In the deepest hole I could find.
I wrote a list of all the bad things in my life
Then tore the paper into tiny pieces.
I collected them in my cupped hands
And blew them across the room
Watching as part of my life floated gently through the air
And fell, helplessly, to the floor.
And when I had swept up the scraps of my past
And hidden them amongst the potato peelings and banana skins
I scrubbed the dregs that still clung tight
Until all that was left was me.

Jeanne Brown

The Fragile Frost

My heart will raise an arctic temple to
 Our love to shrine my tears as frost-burst drops,
Suspended, trembling, strung like captive dew
 On spectral webs . . . where life, life's meaning - stops.
My mind will barricade its shutters to
 The senseless tempest worldly reason brings
And shelter our love's embers - dear - but few -
 Against this savage iced wind's buffetings.
My body will inject grief's floes into
 My nerves to feather our love, tenderly,
With snow - to hibernate desire . . . eschew
 The gnawing ache of wanting you with me.
   But should you choose to shed your warmth again,
   Love may contrive to melt this frozen pain . . .

Barbara Jotham

Change of Form
Dedicated to Rajo Saira - April 1993

Slabs are the stones
Lying, like lotus leaves
On the lake's
Relaxing 's'

The world is a metal bubble
I am a caged mouse
The breeze sighs only against my back

And birdsong
Lands intermittently behind my ears
Cradled by quivering hands.

Prickly feet
Avoid the cool sticky ease of the new-mown grass
In this early April sickness.

By August of next year
Bodies' murmurs have healed
And the red line is written loudly

The 'Danger - High Voltage' sign
Has been dumped in the river
And the flower's stem
Begins the season's stretch

This year is a good one
(No sweets are owed)
It must be a vintage one!

The carved Buddha
Still sits still
And I remember the
Words set in moss-eaten wood:

'From victim to survivor'
And I smile internally
Arms stiff against my aching stomach.

Quibilah Montsho

Untitled

We met, and pledged our love, in June,
oh rapturous July,
passionate love, we made, under an August moon
and a clear September sky.
October, saw our first lover's tiff,
November, fireworks, and if - you think
December, a time of peace and good will,
the new year found us fighting still.
By February, our love was cooling fast
and by the time that March had past,
April's bleak, and showery days,
led us into May - and our separate ways.

Derek Peter Ford

Late Summer

Only the sea remains the same;
curling its lips,
still licks the land to shape.
Even the stones have moved,
disturbed by seeking fingers,
thrown to the greedy waves,
tossed back to lie rootbound
in rocky pools.

I thought that I'd been here before;
a bride in Summer,
building castles,
laughed with babies on the shore.
But it's not so.

Only a stranger briefly glimpsed
over my shoulder,
wearing my flesh.
And when the seagull cries
I fly to scavenge with the birds,
pecking at memories.

Sheila Parry

Alternate Weekends

She leaves them at the gate
unable to endure
the house in which she lived
a few short pregnant months.
He glances slyly as her slender fingers
unconsciously caress the open gate.
The twins run back for yet another kiss.
He stares. He is aware that she is dressed
in this season's gold to complement her hair.
She shudders. Moist tentacles of love
reach out again to stifle her.
He knows the house is womb enticing.
She will eventually return. He waits.
Final farewell's over, impatient to depart
she strides towards the freedom of her car . . .
his gift to her to celebrate the births,
assure her of his love and lure her back.
He leads the boys into the waiting warmth.
He knows she will eventually return
for isn't she the mother of his twins?

Margaret Planeta

Waiting for the Wind

Their life had been a waiting for the wind
Through the long summer days, in sloping meadows,
Where now and then the barest breezes flickered
Across the slumbering ears of corn, like shadows,

And all was still again. Yes, too much silence.
Waiting for winds to set their tall sails turning
And drive the wheels' machinery to churning
And grind the harvest to a smooth white powder.

Water's a ready servant, dammed and herded
Like cattle. And, dumb-beast-like, still obeyed them
As steam. But not the wind. Not tamed. Not captured.
They trusted in its service. It betrayed them.

No more. Today brooks no such patient trusting.
The miller, after a dry windless summer,
Curses the howling gale, and seeks the city,
And steam, and leaves the old mill to its rusting.

Barbara Moss

Walk Over Western Park

Although I knew at any moment
his fingers might accidentally touch mine.
When they did, it electrified
my most intimate thoughts.

Heat so intense my perspiration,
evaporated my mind.
Was it totally innocent
this moment we walked through Western Park.

My answer lay in his denim blue eyes,
Fool that I am, I couldn't bare to look.
Fantasy would end if he held a negative stare.
So I do not glance. Disappointment fills
his hopeful heart. Why doesn't the silly bugger speak?

Sarah Wallace

Exit

'Take your clothes,
your books,
CD's.'
My voice shouts
but my psyche pleads,
'don't go,
it's you I love.
My body needs
our unity.'
Jealousy feeds
with impunity
on doubting minds,
until it finds
the weakest spot
which bleeds.
Then all past deeds
are reiterated.
Anger supersedes
all reason.
Your protestation
stands no chance
against a barrage
of vituperation.
'You fornicating boor!'
Yet all the time
my mind begs 'stay',
but while I search for words
you pick up your possessions
and leaving
slam the door.

Liz Yule

Lovers Quarrel

It was easy for you to say ' I love you',
But not to vilify me.
It was easy for you to steal my heart.
But not to shatter the things we share.
It was easy for you to put the ring on my finger,
But not to break the circle of togetherness.
It was easy for you to open the door, and tell me not to linger,
But not to shower me with words of hate and malice.
It was easy for you to take away our other part
But you forget the ties of emotion are stronger.
It was easy for you to say
I do not want you any longer.
It was easy for you to close your eyes.
But if you do not see my face
Then all our world dies.

Arthur E Magnus

Sorry

If every word we said was written down,
If every face we pulled became a painting on the wall,
How long before we listened to the other side,
Before we realise we didn't know it all.

The snarl across a room can never show a saddened heart,
The ranting screaming lies just hide the truth,
The burning desire to be the last to come apart,
Leaves only desolation.

To take you in my arms and say 'I'm sorry' could be played back every day
with the backing of guitar,
To learn to read between the lines and to say ' I didn't mind',
Would turn the raging beast into a movie star.

So now I say 'I'm sorry' and things never were as bad as the monster said they were yesterday,
And I'm listening to the real you now and I hope that I can give my best performance in this marriage play.

Simon Kay

Midnight

Midnight, and I've
Gone to bed,
Without switching
Off the lights.

Too scared,
To stay awake
And keep the nightmares away,
Now the family's gone.

Christopher Booth

A Prickly Relationship - Fading Fast

You wanted flowers so I brought you flowers.
You had asked for flowers
but you'd wanted special flowers - roses.
So I got you roses.
Roses - cut, beheaded, sheared - you didn't want,
for roses such as these soon die.
You wanted plants, rose plants,
the living rose.
I found you rose plants,
but they took some time to bloom - as roses do -
and had no scent,
no perfume for the night.
Some roses are like that;
they sacrifice their smell for shape.
You failed to be impressed.
You like old-fashioned roses
and you claimed I should have known.
How could I know? You never said.
I got more rose plants anyway -
old-fashioned roses.
Great surprise! You loved the scent,
the scent of yesterdays for you I never knew.
You didn't like the colours.
So I dug up all the scented roses,
bought new in the colours you desired
and planted them to form a solid semicircle
just six feet above where I had planted you.

Adrian Jones

Lammas

You put our love story
into a poem
and read that poem
to our writing class!

At school, you outstripped me
in brashness and lust,
yet envied my brain;
is this your revenge -

to write a poem on 'Partings'
dedicated to me,
sanctioning your desertion,
exposing my disguise?

In impeccable rhetoric, now,
you rest your case,
discounting my defence
as stench-reeking lies.

Before the eve of Lammas,
time of harvest and chaos,
I return your accusations,
ripped into tiny shreds.

Eamer O'Keeffe

Love in Mind

Constant warmth enfolding lover's moods soon flown:
Two eager sticks rubbed hard to full arousal
Hungry flames consuming brittle life
Blisters burnt amid foul acrid smoke
Blown apart as embers die
- a sigh as I retreat.

In solitude a beckoning back of warmth
Sweet girlish glow denied by passion's ram
Alive, alone and licking wounds: saliva heals
Spins a gauze of love - a smile
Serenely curled around
The contours of my mind.

Brenda Dove

Susanna in Kaleidoscope

You sat in sun between the vines
Flake of gold, fields of
Littered hay,
Mines
Of open casting, veins
Of stretching day,
Your prisms parting into severed lines

Deflecting broken sun,
Patched quilt,
A spray
Of shards, none
Intact but near,
Jigsaws of a briefest day,
That ends yet never seems quite done.

Much like the Dead have seen
But could not hoard,
Left where
Days shatter as we grow unseen.
Crossing borders is a must
And snapping cords - yet we will share
What will be and has always been.

Part of parting and farewells.

Robert Gregory Bishop

Once Again

You walk away from me,
Footfalls of sunlight
Disappearing
As my shadow swallows
Me whole again.

The circumference of
Darkness
As my outline
Becomes solitary
once again.

You walk away from me
Nothing more to be said
Laughter waiting in another's eyes
Yet to be woken
By your smile again.

There are tracks
Where you feet have fallen.
Hungry I crawl into them
Following, watching you
Searching, once again.

V M Anne Jones

Untitled

It doesn't really matter now
Buried six feet deep and trampled with dirt
No longer pre-occupied
With the whys, the whens, the buts, the hurt.

You didn't have to lie to me
I made enough excuses for two
Though in frustration I'd shout your name
But you were only there when it suited you.

A sponge to soak your troubles and burdens
I fulfilled your selfish sexual desire
While you abused my love, my body
You abused my mind, my soul, my character.

I thought I'd never love again
Why looking back it made no sense
Time is the healer, I believe it now
From love, to hate, to anger, to indifference.

Verena West

The Masochist

A hinted farewell in a tattered room predicted
Brash words of justification hurriedly scrawled at a rented table.
And dustless gaps on shelves revealed to sympathisers
That domesticity had been of small priority
In the days and nights of our premature co-habitation.

In airlessness of summer and its overly long light tedium
I dared to crawl into the happy vale of others
To disappoint, depress and deviate
From their predetermined stages of my recovery.
The world reviles the hapless masochist.

Denise Lee

Nightime Rain

The rain ran down the windows
distorting the street outside
into a variety of shapes and patterns.
She sat by the window,
positioning herself to see
both the clock and the door.
Occasionally she would stir
the unwanted coffee,
an automatic reaction to her tension.

For what seemed like the hundredth time
she cleared a small area
of condensation from the window,
and looked out into the night.
The proprietor busied himself
with unnecessary jobs,
knowing no words of his were needed.

Eventually with a sigh
and a glance at the clock,
he flipped the *open* sign to *closed*.
His eyes met hers in silence.
Reluctantly she rose
wrapping her coat round herself
and lifting the suitcase from the floor.

At the door she turned
and he thought he could see
the nightime rain running down her face.
She stepped out into the night
and slowly walked away.
He watched her go
into the shadows of the night.

Howard Atkinson

April Sixth and April Seventh

April sixth, flowers were in full bloom
while the sun shone intermittently.
I was happy I never suspected a thing
well not until that unexpected ring.

She stood there nervously with a smile
almost pitiful like a child.
I recognised her face
but somehow it couldn't be placed.
She jogged my memory recalling events four years ago.
That was the time I remember that you were
itching and tempted to roam.
I thought that was the past
but it seems that the past has come full circle at last.

She spoke quietly and slowly
almost in fear of re-approachment.
I listened attentively
absorbed and spellbound by her sadness and pain.
How could she come here, I thought
does she have no shame.

She paused briefly for a while
then the bombshell dropped
that she had a child.
What did she want from me
I was devastated couldn't she see?

I had to ask her to leave
because somehow I needed a reprieve.
I think she left without saying a word
by that time all sounds were muffled and unheard.

April seventh - the sun shines
but for me . . . I'll close the blinds . . .

Lorreene Hunte

Sad Face

The condensation
On the window
Formed a face,
A sad, sad face.
So sad in fact
That whilst I watched
It cried real tears.

Tony Jones

Father's Day

Your face just like the weather
set and grey
you wait upon the step
not much to say . . .

Get back before it grows
too damp and dark -
they'll need a bath
when they've been out all Sunday
in the park

I'll finish ironing
once you're through the gate
and dampen it with tears
of love and hate -
and then I'll reminisce for quite a while
wrapped in our former loving warm lifestyle;
so many things I'm going to miss -
your laughter and your humour
good night - kiss

We'd lie down by the flames
of our coal-fire
(what happened to that closeness -
that desire?)
the children safe and happy
tucked in bed -
Are all the embers now completely dead?

How did we come to drift so far apart -
no reconciliation - no fresh start?

It was a party
I got drunk for Heaven's sake -
I'm *not* a tart.

Joan Bulmer

A Winter in My Heart

Ice hangs like lace on window panes
The lake a frozen mirror.
Wild birds have left the hedgerow wall
I feel the chill and shiver.

This is the feeling now you've gone
A winter in my heart,
Always you were the only one
Cold tears I held now start.

Remember once the sunny days
Down lanes with Mayflower sweet.
Your loving touch your gentle ways
That turned to passion heat.

We cooled our passion by the lake
Made love beneath the sun
And then my hand you gently take
Saying love has just begun.

But that seems very long ago
Or was it yesterday,
When you had said you had to go
And I had begged you stay.

I begged you stay for just a while
And held on to you tight.
You held me close and gave a smile
But crept away that night.

Mary Jones

Trinity

I could listen to your voice and split it into three:
The depths are probing, uncertain, doubtful
Mid-range to strangers, off hand but sure
High level, ecstatic, silly, hateful -

Yet I heard your voice and desired you
Like a vial of oil over my chapped feet
Weary from chasing your caprice.

I gave up one who I understood
Loved, even, to be sacrificed
In your labyrinth of contradictions

While the conundrum of myself
Has been reduced to a sentiment:
I loathe you,
The you in me.

Greta Brickell

The Target

I'm the target you use
to practise on.
Your mouth is full of buckshot
as you aim carelessly
then pepper me with your frustrations.
Sometimes you hit the spot,
sometimes you miss,
sometimes a ricochet takes you by surprise.

A cease-fire is needed,
dialogue is the only way out,
close communication with the adversary,
but you say that would hurt too much
and pick up your gun once again.

Pippa McCathie

Golden Web

Once you spun
A golden web
With strands
Drawn from the sun.
Now all that's left
Is the rusting thread
My remains
Are hanging from.

Brian Covell

Cardiac Arrest

They sat in opposing seats,
The cards were on the table,
Indubitably so.
Trumping his King she spoke
Quietly, adamantly.
I'm leaving you for him.

White gleamed his knuckles,
Fingers gripping edge of table.
Trollop, he snarled,
Eyes glinting sudden hatred.
Her blatant admission
Left him soulless.

They noted the upended table,
Her body lay blood soaked.
Gruesome sight,
Cards scattered around,
Handle of a knife protruding,
Penetrating deep through the Ace of Hearts.

James Ashman

A Vermilion Pool

The knife goes in - one cut is all it took
The blood spills out - it is bright red
Although you would have called it vermilion.

It was because you used words like vermilion
that you had to go
You were so much better than me
and you didn't let me forget it.

I'll never forget the look on your face
The wide open mouth, the look of disbelief
But I did it. And now you lie bubbling
in a pool of vermilion blood.

Siân Headon

Normal Service Will be Resumed as Soon as Possible

Last night was the final straw
I cannot tolerate any more
Sitting, watching endless television
I may as well be in Holloway prison.
Am I finding excuses for a love that has died
Too stupid to accept it or just too full of pride.

How can feelings change overnight
When yesteryear marriage was all right.
I rushed out of work in anticipation
My heart beating with wild palpitation.
Eager to find his face in the crowd
My arm through his, I felt wonderfully proud.

The test of time has shown
His lack of interest in having fun.
Television was the love of his life
And second-best reserved for his wife.
His eyes were permanently glued to the screen
My revealing décolletage went totally unseen.

I may as well have worn a black bin liner
Or been covered in soot like a Yorkshire miner.
The only way of making an impression
On my husband's permanent obsession
Would be to appear on the nine o'clock news,
Or take a course on 'How to change a Fuse'!

Last night I told him we had to divorce
Between Emmerdale and Inspector Morse
Nannette Newman was commencing to squirt
Washing-up liquid in her latest advert
Then came the girl with the Cadbury flakes
I left in a hurry for both of our sakes.

Joy Adams

Lady Stopped Loving Me

I see a lady walking in the city,
Clicking her high heels on the street,
I see a lady walking past my window,
Wiping her brow from the heavy heat,
I see a lady that I once knew,
Happy and content without me, oh,
I see a lady who I've touched under a sheet,
But now she doesn't want me, no.

I see a lady turn to walk for my door,
She's been this way many times before,
I see a lady try to walk on by,
Not wishing to enter, not sure,
I see a lady her heart hurt, she stops,
Hoping I'm not in. I whisper 'beware',
I see my lady, her face drops,
Realising, I'm still there.

Stuart Lancaster

Cain's Answer

You put the mark of Cain upon my forehead,
named me Judas with a kiss,
destroyed yourself to punish me,
was not enough
to make me lifetime servant to your hate,
you poisoned those I love.

Tearing my flesh in strips
would fail your longing for revenge,
and only in the shredding of my mind
would you exult.
But I shall fight,
and never satisfy your need.

My soul is mine.

Carole Carr

Breaking Up

I slept in the railway station
My body wracked with pain
When I thought of my darling loved one
Whom I'd never see again.

I am alone and wand'ring
But I'd rather leave this life
Than settle in the humdrum ways again
Amid this world of war and strife.

For Fate took him away from me
And now I'm on my own
My friends have all forsaken me
I dream of the love I have known.

I haunt the rubbish tips and scrapyards
In hopes I can find something to eat
The wine in my bottle has gone stale
And weariness attacks my feet.

And now with that good life I'm done
And although I know it seems
That I'm wasting my nights and days
I still have my golden precious dreams.

I bear my troubles and grief now
With a heart that's growing so weak
I'm weary of these thoughts of remembrance
And now 'tis happiness I seek.

And what is there to give my joy
In a world void of peace and love
I'll let the sun shine down on me
Knowing that one day we'll meet again Above.

Mary Hayworth

For He Who Waits

They walk apart, no hand must touch.
She looks that way, he looks this.
Speak to all their friends, never to each other.
Never smile, or crack a joke
For themselves to laugh together.
We see the sorrow as their love
Just flounders in the wind.
Like a sad and weary butterfly
Fluttering vainly to stay aloft.
Her face is tired, and his the same.
What sweet revenge I take
From remembering the dazzling smiles
On the day she ran to him.

Ted Harrison

Wild Rose

Wild Rose, your untamed beauty I do crave,
E'en though I know in time sweet scent will fade -
Your womanly charms I will help preserve,
For Love's sake, autumn's grave you shall evade.
Come, let me pluck you in your prime my Queen;
Let me fetch divine water from life's spring
So you may drink to remain evergreen;
At least, till we hear Winter's Robin sing.
Now let breath blow strong from glassblower's lips,
Twist molten glass; keep one end held fix'd:
Shape the fine vase with skilful fingertips -
For that crimson empress whom I hand pick'd!
  Wild Rose, may you rest at your graceful best,
    Safe, from Time - who wouldst thy beauty molest.

Thomas M Ryder

Words

Words are like weapons
They can damage and maim,
Cutting and killing as they
fly through the air.
Spiteful and hurtful, such damage
they cause,
Shafts dripping with poison, can't
be recalled;
No visible mark do they leave
when they land,
The damage they cause, one cannot see;
but, damage there is, and long after
it shows
When what was once love, ends
with these words.

Margaret Sparvell

Already Naked

You have moved away,
already naked to
other hands and mouths.

I made wrong assumptions
about the colour of your hair.
My secrets have been emptied
out in public places.

My blood is black.
My filth will never be forgiven.
At last I can shit in your mouth.

Chris Kenworthy

Recollection

To get me out of the house
you offered my services
as overnight babysitter for your friend.
I didn't know your plans
The moment my back was turned
you collected my friend.

In our bedroom, in our bed
you provided your services
You didn't clean the room, leaving traces
of stale sweat and semen
That scent poisoned my return.
I collected my cases.

Anne Stewart

Tampering

Winter's frost, a natural thing,
Breaks up the soil to tilth the Spring.
Sun's atoms splitting solar mass
Give heat to succour Summer's grass.
Man husbands Nature's fruitful wealth,
So, Man ensures Man's future health.

Yet lust, mingling in his selfish mirth,
With heedless seed produces birth.
Its creature's natural needs cast out
Love's tender germ, no time to sprout.
White-hot kisses chilled, ne'er fond,
Sever soon the fragile bond.

The secrets of the Universe
Tempt Man to scorn the hidden curse
Of power to make him one with God.
His atom-tinkering shapes the rod
To break the backs of decades hence.

O, wilful Man, where is the sense?
Spent cores will radiate a strength
To contaminate beyond the length
Of your life-span, bringing doom
To generations still to womb.

Fragmentation scientific,
No breaking-up is more specific!

Don Smith

How Deep My Love

At last, the all important day,
Beside the Altar hand in hand
our vows we made: they're meant to stay
from this time forth, And thus they stand
the covenant we've made

And as between the sheets for hours
those many nights we romped and played.
Your body lithesome as a flower
entwined with mine that wondrous way
uniting both with power.

And through it all we spoke of love,
so meaningful as from the soul.
Such happiness as from above,
feelings remote, beyond control.
My love, my love, my love.

Was it, alas, the lack of will
blindly insisting that we part?
And was there nothing more to fill
the empty void within our hearts?
Now gone those early thrills.

Those cries of love, distant yet close.
Was it true love, or sex which posed
as love? Romantic sex which dreams
so short a time, then goes.

Parting . . . What memories are left?
Sex, so triumphant leaves a need
for something more. An ache bereft.
In truth, it must be love we heed.
Sex, love, both warp and weft.

Collin West

Smileless

Smileless,
Hungerless,
Thirstless,
Friendless,

Laughless,
Thoughtless'
Careless,
Loveless,

Joyless,
Sleepless
Lifeless,
You less.

Kim Davies

Walls

Goodbye, you shouted, slamming the door.
The sound ricocheted
Around the walls
As though I stood in a large bare room.

How strange,
Because the flat is small,
Lounge, bed and bath,
Compact, the Agent said.

Time was its walls
Surrounded us with warmth.
Our laughter chimed about them,
Our happiness lit them.

Now I'm alone,
And echoing walls stand high.

Gladys M Green

Goodwill Message

You went out like a snapped cracker,
On Christmas Day,
Too quickly for goodbyes
Or exchanged presents;
Too quickly to tell you I understood
The male teasing,
The easy tactlessness;
Too quickly to regret
My sharp touchiness,
The opposition
For opposition's sake;
The sometimes rudeness.

Ten years later,
Writing a novel
In bursts and stops,
A character emerged
Sympathetically you,
As if I wanted to proffer
In love
The present I thought I'd lost.

Jennifer Holland

David's Plight

David's plight was common
yet unique to him.
He was alone
lonely and
homeless.
His wife died
crossing the road:
his world crumbled.
The light switched off
depression held his mind.
Nothing mattered -
when she had gone.
He cursed his body
for its demands,
his mind for its remembering.
David was thirty-nine -
the span from
Queen Victoria's death
to Hitler's war -
but in another time.
David died
in a shop doorway
on a cold March night.

Peter Cranswick

Disappointment

Gain solitude within a mirrored darkness
That calms your soul.
Lock yourself in a timeless
Motionless spell and anything can happen.
But don't be fooled it could just be
A mirage or maybe just a reflection from behind
Which is far removed from your situation.
This is called disappointment.

Chinedu

Love's Victims

Fellow sufferer, in me confide
        that which you conceal from the world outside.
Brothers and sisters - victims in love's game
        united in sorrow and feelings of pain.
We gave our trust, so heartlessly broken;
we gave our love, with words truly spoken.

Foolish schemes, built on unfulfilled dreams,
        but the memories will stay,
                'til our dying day.
Did we imagine those special moments we shared,
        those little tokens,
                to say that we cared?

John Jolley